Mass Unemployment

The Royer Lectures

Series editor: John M. Letiche, University of
California, Berkeley

Mass Unemployment

Edmond Malinvaud

Basil Blackwell

© Edmond Malinvaud 1984

First published 1984

Basil Blackwell Publisher Ltd
108 Cowley Road, Oxford OX4 1JF, UK

Basil Blackwell Inc.
432 Park Avenue South, Suite 1505,
New York, NY 10016, USA

British Library Cataloguing in Publication Data

Malinvaud, Edmond
    Mass unemployment.—(The Royer lectures)
    I. Title   II. Series
    331.13'7   HD5705.5

    ISBN 0—631—13704—1

Typeset by Cambrian Typesetters, Aldershot, Hants
Printed in Great Britain by Billings & Son Ltd, Worcester

Bst

 # 17. 95

Contents

Foreword

Written in a clear, crisp, and persuasive style, this superb book was prepared for a general as well as a professional audience. For many years, Professor Edmond Malinvaud has served as Director of the National Institute of Statistics and Economic Studies in France. He has exceptional talents of theoretical insight, detailed empirical knowledge, and extensive policy experience. In this book he brings these attributes to bear on a diagnosis, marshalling of evidence, and treatment of mass unemployment in developed market economies.

With encompassing brevity, he has provided a fresh appraisal not only of the unemployment issue, but of the design and implementation of macroeconomic research and policy. The book is in three parts. Part 1 contains a masterly description of the unemployment problem confronting the western world. It effectively criticizes the classical tradition in economics, which virtually assumes away the problem. Part 2 usefully extends Malinvaud's earlier work, as expressed principally in *The Theory of Unemployment Reconsidered* (1977) and *Profitability and Unemployment* (1980), on the distinction between Keynesian and classical unemployment and the role of *profitability* in determining economic growth. Part 3 discusses policy conclusions that can be drawn, either firmly or tentatively, from the earlier analysis. It includes the international implications of new forms of protectionism in coping with

mass unemployment as a lasting, disequilibrium phenomenon.

According to Malinvaud, the two major currents of
macroeconomics – the neo-Keynesian and the market-
clearing approaches – have proven inadequate as explanatory systems of contemporary mass unemployment. An
examination of actual cases shows that such unemployment is often associated with profitability, and not only in
the short term. From 1973 to 1983, in the industrial
countries of Europe, actual and anticipated increases in
production costs lowered the growth rate of the demand
for labor. As real wages were more inflexible downward in
Great Britain, France and Germany than in the United
States, the absolute level of unemployment in these
European countries continually increased; while in the
United States it did indeed rise during periods of economic
contraction, it fell markedly during periods of economic
expansion.

Most of the observed disequilibrium, Malinvaud
contends, was in the price system, though it was related, of
course, to macroeconomic trends. The effects of changes
in the price aggregates, especially of those in the real wage
and in the real rate of interest, were of major significance.
The law of supply and demand operated slowly at this
economic level. To an increasing degree the extent to
which the aggregate supply of labor in different countries
had to adjust was related to classical macroeconomic
conditions rather than to neo-Keynesian macroeconomic
conditions. While Keynes had placed major emphasis on
short-term insufficient effective demand as causing mass
unemployment, under contemporary conditions Malinvaud places more emphasis on longer-term rising costs and
decreased profitability as causing insufficient capital
formation and. therefore, mass unemployment even in
periods of relatively high capacity utilization. Malinvaud

believes that the integration of more general microeconomic and macroeconomic analysis should help to
explain why the adjustments in both labor and capital
markets have not been more rapid, or more effectively
oriented to each other.

In one of the most original and cogent discussions of the
lectures, Malinvaud considers ways in which key relative
prices that have been distorted in an economy might be
corrected. The section entitled "Actions on Prices, Incomes
and Costs" (pages 81–94), sets forth a research program
regarding these factors. It draws attention, however, to the
requirement and means of improving both the technical
apparatus and the data base for more effective policy
formulation. Attendant upon his own suggestions for
research are the following. (1) There is an important need
for further work on the determinants of the size of the
labor force in the United States and Western Europe. In
papers by K.B. Clark and L.H. Summers (cited on pages
31 and 33), it was shown that in the United States about
half of all unemployment periods end in labor-force with-
drawal. Discouraged workers are clearly an important issue
in American mass unemployment. Similar problems may
be related to mass unemployment among European
immigrant workers. (2) Relations between oil shocks,
worldwide productivity decline, and mass unemployment
will doubtless require further examination, Malinvaud
suggests. He refers to these significant interrelations and
suggests avenues for further research. Nonetheless, in the
context of models with which he works, including non-
malleable technology, such exogenous shocks could have
powerful effects on the conclusions derived. (3) Malinvaud
devotes attention to the need for comparative research on
the effects in some countries of downward real-wage in-
flexibility. The contrasts between the operation of certain
labor markets, and especially the relative success of Japan

and the United States as compared with the major countries of Western Europe in containing mass unemployment certainly demands further scrutiny.

Members of the Department of Economics at the University of California at Berkeley are pleased to have had Professor Edmond Malinvaud, an economist of truly international distinction, deliver the 1983 Royer Lectures upon which this book is based. We believe that the reader will share our gratitude for the author's careful preparation of these lectures and our obligation to the publishers for expediting publication.

JOHN M. LETICHE

Acknowledgement

These lectures were given at the University of California at Berkeley in October 1983 as the Royer Lectures. I benefited greatly in their preparation from discussions at Berkeley and from suggestions made by P. Dubois, B. Grais, J. Letiche, R. Salais and R. Turvey, to whom my thanks.

Introduction

Unemployment is high throughout North America and Western Europe, but economists seem by and large to behave as if they no longer believe they can do much about it. The fact that the general public feel this to be so raises a disturbing question: is it really true that economists can no longer propose policies capable of reducing mass unemployment?

Let us admit from the start that as economists we are much less self-confident than we were twenty years ago. Developments since then have shown the deficiencies of policies we used to advocate. We have realized that, under certain circumstances, the problem of unemployment has turned out to be much more stubborn than we thought.

We know that mass unemployment is mainly an economic phenomenon, since it results from the functioning of the economic system. Moreover, we know that mass unemployment deeply affects the whole fabric of society and is for that reason a major social problem. Even if we do not say so we also know that this problem directly concerns us and that one of our most important functions as economists is to clarify the necessary conditions for its resolution. The complexity of the problem is not a valid excuse for neglecting to study it.

This very complexity, added to our misgivings about our earlier treatment of the subject, suggest that what is needed is a complete reconsideration of it. We should not, of course, expect to discover essentially new lines of approach that would give us the power we lack at present to tackle mass unemployment. But we need to sort out, to check, to revise and to extend our ideas on the subject. We must assure ourselves that some of our previous knowledge is sound. We must identify points on which we ought to proceed to new investigations. We must reconsider and perhaps rebuild our theories. We should probably set up new econometric models. Finally, we must think over specific policies and discover how to better serve our countries in their search for a way out of their present difficulties.

I can, of course, not pretend to cover this long agenda here. Nor can I pretend that we are near to coping with it, notwithstanding a good deal of new research. But I have, during these lectures, surveyed the subject in my own way. The plan they follow is quite natural: the first lecture discusses the many dimensions of the phenomenon of mass unemployment, the second considers the macroeconomic theoretical analysis of it, and the third explores ways in which economists could be more helpful when policies are to be chosen.

The reader should, however, be warned that I do not claim these three lectures are three successive steps in the discovery of a solution to our present problems. My purpose is, indeed, not to advocate a solution but to convey the outcome of my experience and reflections. These are multifarious and cover a wide spectrum, from fundamental theory to economic policy; they do not result in a well-integrated whole.

In particular, I do not claim that what I state about policies during the third lecture can be proved to be valid by rigorous application of the theoretical framework that is proposed in the second. Indeed, I shall even stress that my theoretical research concerns the exploratory stage in the development of a conceptual apparatus and that many further stages have to be carefully studied before anyone can confidently rely upon this apparatus. At the present time, discussions about policies must either apply already familiar and well-tested models or, by necessity, be openly heuristic.

Each one of the three lectures has, then, a distinct and autonomous purpose. The first one considers why mass unemployment should be treated as a disequilibrium. The second presents my views on the development of the macroeconomic theory of unemployment. In the third one, I try to convey my analysis of the lack of success of economic policies in maintaining full employment; this analysis, of course, draws on my experience with Western European, and particularly French, problems.

The reader must understand that these lectures are silent on aspects of the unemployment problem that are too specific to be relevant for the progress of general economic knowledge. They cover topics on which new research seems to be particularly needed and ideas that, while perhaps still debatable, are worthy of wider examination and, eventually, of diffusion.

1 The Phenomenon

For economists the phenomenon of mass unemployment is a disequilibrium, namely an excess of the supply of labor over the demand for it. In order to grasp this phenomenon, before beginning to analyze it, we must of course start from the available statistics. But we cannot take them as measuring exactly what we want. We must proceed to some preliminary analysis in order to check that there is indeed a disequilibrium, beyond the normal rotation of people in-between two jobs, or the normal search time for new intrants into the labor force. In other words, we must identify the disequilibrium component of unemployment which is not directly given by the statistics.

A little reflection explains why current statistics do not break down unemployment between frictional and disequilibrium unemployment. Indeed, the distinction is, to a large extent, conventional and no agreement has so far been reached on which convention should be adopted. Since statistics are meant to be objective and to rely on commonly agreed concepts and principles, the time has not yet come, and perhaps will never come, when frictional unemployment is regularly evaluated by official statisticians.

In order to set the scene for the two following lectures, I shall first give a brief look at the published statistics, then discuss the distinction between frictional and disequilibrium unemployment. This will naturally lead us to inquire how some unemployment may exist above that which can be considered to be frictional. Since the existence of this type of unemployment is sometimes disputed nowadays, we shall, finally, have to study the proofs that can be given of it.

What is Unemployment?

Unemployment statistics apply a definition that has progressively emerged as being the most appropriate for modern economies. It does not directly follow from a literal interpretation of the word, but rather from the concern with some social and policy issues. The process that led to this definition involved many people and meetings, in particular the Eighth and Thirteenth International Conferences of Labor Statisticians (ILO, Geneva, 1954 and 1982) and President John F. Kennedy's Committee to Appraise Employment and Unemployment Statistics (1961).[1]

In their definition of employment, statisticians now refer only to gainful occupation, as distinguished from work being done for one's own satisfaction or for the care of one's family. On the other hand, they do not count as unemployed all those who are not working for gain but only those who are not so working but would like to.

This principle does not precisely determine the number

---

[1] This committee was chaired by the late Aaron Gordon who was teaching at Berkeley.

For a brief history of employment and unemployment as statistical concepts see, for instance, National Commission on Employment and Unemployment Statistics, *Counting the Labor Force* (Washington, 1979), chapter 2. The latest international recommendations concerning the measurement of unemployment were agreed at the 1982 conference of labor statisticians and are given in *Bulletin of Labor Statistics* 3 (1983).

of unemployed. Its application would be subject to a large margin of uncertainty if it were not further codified. In particular, we have to decide exactly when someone is considered as wishing to work. The requirement is that he or she must be actively looking for a job, maybe only a part-time one, but a job to be taken straight away. The notion of "actively looking" is, however, not too strictly interpreted since only one move during the preceding month is usually required, the move being, for instance, to visit a potential employer, to write a letter of application or to inquire at a labor exchange office.

I shall not discuss here how these rules and the international recommendations concerning them are applied in different countries, all of which face particular difficulties of one type or another. Suffice it to say that statistics from different countries are never rigorously comparable, that the degree of harmonization between most OECD countries is progressively improving, but that the US Bureau of Labor Statistics and the OECD Secretariat still find it necessary to amend a number of national figures in order to provide analysts and research workers with unemployment rates that are, at least roughly, comparable from one country to another.

The broad facts are well known. First and foremost, unemployment varies through time and from one country or region to another. This is clear as soon as we look at existing data on the unemployment rate, i.e. the ratio between the number of unemployed and the number of people in the labor force.

In the USA, for instance, during the last forty years, the unemployment rate has experienced many fluctuations, which appear on the series of annual averages, even though this series partly smoothes out the peaks and troughs (see figure 1). In France, which may be taken as an example for the European countries that have undergone a significantly

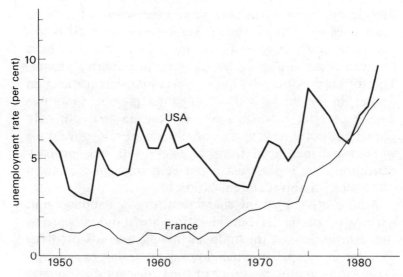

FIGURE 1 Unemployment rates in the USA and France

different evolution, the unemployment rate remained lower than 2 per cent from 1949 to 1968; since then it has increased in successive waves, up to 8 per cent and more in 1982 and 1983. The figures for the year 1982 also show a substantial variation in unemployment rates between Western European countries, with 6 per cent in Western Germany, 9 in Italy, 10 in the Netherlands, 13 in the United Kingdom and Belgium, and 16 in Spain.[2]

It is also well known that unemployment rates vary between sociodemographic groups, according to a pattern

---

[2] Figures for the USA are taken from US Government Printing Office, *Economic Report of the President* (Washington, 1983). They concern unemployment as a percentage of the civilian labor force. For France the rate is a percentage of the total labor force; figures are taken from INSEE, *Le mouvement économique en France, 1949–1979* (Paris, 1981) and INSEE, *Rapport sur les comptes de la nation, année 1982* (Paris, 1983). OECD figures have been quoted for other countries.

that seems to be about the same everywhere in modern economies and at all times. These rates are particularly high for young people, for women, for those who have received little education and for racial minority groups. The differences may be quite substantial. For instance in France, in the spring of 1982, the unemployment rate was 33 per cent for women aged less than 25 and with only primary education; it was 9 and 5 per cent respectively for women and men aged from 25 to 49 with only primary education; but it was just 2 per cent for men aged from 25 to 49 with university education.[3]

Among other relevant characteristics of unemployment, worthy of particular consideration are those concerning the distribution of unemployed people according to the duration of the spell of unemployment that they experience. Observation at any one point of time does not directly give this distribution. What can be recorded is the time at which each unemployed person entered his or her current spell of employment but we do not know when this will end. A reliable model can, however, be built up of the relationship linking the two relevant statistical distributions: the distribution of spells of unemployment according to their duration and the distribution of the unemployed according to the time they have already spent in their current spell of employment. Observation of the second distribution permits a good estimate of the first.

Such an estimation has been made by various research workers, for instance for France and the USA.[4] It has been

---

[3] See M. Cézard, N. Coëffic and P. Laulhé, "L'enquête emploi rénovée," *Economie et Statistique* (January 1983).

[4] See, in particular, R. Salais, "Chômage: fréquences d'entrée et durées moyennes selon l'enquête emploi," *Annales de l'INSEE* 16–17 (May–December 1974); K.B. Clark and L.H. Summers, "Labor market dynamics and unemployment: a reconsideration," *Brookings Papers on Economic Activity* (no. 1, 1979).

found that the curve showing the distribution of unemployment duration tends to have a typical shape, which seems to apply fairly universally, in different countries, at different times and even for the various population subgroups that we may want to identify. This shape is given by a continuous distribution whose density decreases from high values for short spells of unemployment and which has, however, a rather fat and long tail before it becomes negligible.

This typical shape looks like that of an exponential distribution. But its tail is fatter. An exponential distribution would imply that the probability of getting out of unemployment was independent of the time already spent unemployed but, in fact, this probability decreases as the length of the spell of unemployment increases. The mathematical form of the distribution is then closer to that of a Weibull law, which would exactly apply if the probability of leaving unemployment decreased as a power function of the time already spent unemployed. Such a pattern was found in the two estimates, by Salais, and Clark and Summers quoted above. More recent work by Salais on other French data confirms this, except for very long spells of unemployment when the probability of leaving unemployment might be still smaller.[5] (See figure 2 which, however, comes from data on registered unemployment and so does not exactly apply the ILO definition of unemployment.)

This typical shape means that many of those who experienced unemployment did so only for short spells (at least for most of the times they experienced it). But it also means that, among those unemployed at any one time, a good many will remain in this situation for a fairly long

---

[5] R. Salais, "Le chômage: un phénomène de file d'attente," *Economie et Statistique* (July 1980).

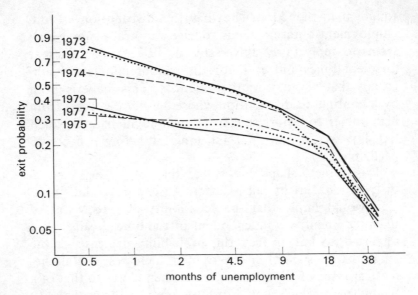

FIGURE 2 The probability of leaving unemployment as a function of
time spent unemployed (for men in France; log scale)

period. When thinking about unemployment, then, we
must remember that many people will find a job or give up
the search rather quickly, and that many other unemployed
people will have the feeling of waiting in a rather long
queue.

When economic conditions vary, the probability of
leaving unemployment also varies for each group of unemployed people. So far as one can now infer from available results, it varies in the same way for all groups. For
instance, it rises for all when employment in industry
increases.[6] This also means that, although it always has

---

[6] Changes of the parameters of the Weibull distribution have been
found to be well explained by a few aggregate variables. See Salais,
Economie et Statistique (1980).

and considering, therefore, a phenomenon that appears at the most aggregated level, I shall consider this structural unemployment as being part of frictional unemployment (indeed, if there was absolutely no mismatch of any sort, there would be no frictional unemployment, except during the process of bargaining for the wage rate). On the other hand, "structural unemployment" is also used to refer to the aggregate phenomenon due to a deficiency of the labor requirement of the stock of existing profitable equipment with respect to the supply of labor. It is then part of disequilibrium unemployment and will be termed "classical unemployment" in my second lecture. (OECD have recently used the terminology "equipment deficient unemployment.")

Even if we stick to the frictional–disequilibrium dichotomy, we must recognize that the distinction between the two components is not clear. When should we speak of an equilibrium in the labor market, unemployment being then purely frictional? There is no obvious answer, and for good reason.

Equilibrium is an abstract notion, which explicitly or implicitly refers to some theoretical scheme. Economists tend to define it by reference to supply and demand. We then say that the labor market is in equilibrium if, at the prevailing wage rate, the supply of labor is equal to the demand for labor. But the labor market is not homogeneous: there are as many markets as there are relevant geographical areas and labor qualifications. To talk of equilibrium in the labor market is, therefore, to consider the average situation; it is not to claim that excess supply or demand could exist nowhere.

Moreover, there are differing views on what equilibrium is in the market for any good or service. Sellers would like to see buyers take the first offer made to them; they complain that they must bear the cost of expensive advertising campaigns. Buyers, on the other hand, often think that they do not easily find exactly what they want and that supply does not meet their demand. Similarly, employers will always point to difficulties they face in recruiting at least part of their staff, while workers will feel that the market is not favorable enough for them.

Where exactly we should draw the line between frictional and disequilibrium unemployment can, then, only be decided by convention. But a conventional distinction is not a useless one. Quite the contrary. As long as the convention is known and used consistently through space and time, it may considerably help to organize our thoughts about the phenomena under examination.

Most of what I say here does not depend on precisely where the line is drawn. It depends only on the observation that, for any feasible and sensible convention, disequilibrium in the labor market changes through time and space. Its changes therefore require an explanation that cannot come from any theoretical framework assuming equality between demand and supply. Similarly, if we have to discuss policy measures intended to act on mass unemployment, such a theoretical framework cannot be appropriate.

In order to avoid confusion, let me point out that the rate of frictional unemployment, i.e. the ratio of this type of unemployment to the labor force, has no necessary relationship to what has been called the "natural rate of unemployment" or NAIRU — the "non-accelerating inflation rate of unemployment." These concepts have appeared as convenient analytical tools in some theories of the inflationary process. They will not concern us here, except for some quite marginal references on occasion when we shall have to consider changes of the price level. For the main part, our problem will be to explain disequilibrium unemployment and to study ways of reducing it, but not to inquire about its consequences on other economic variables, except when some feedback relation from these variables to unemployment will have to be taken into account.[9]

We should, moreover, note that the unemployment rate, as recorded in the statistics, does not necessarily provide the best measure of tightness of the labor market, i.e. the best measure of the direction and degree of disequilibrium in this market. The ratio of frictional unemployment to the labor force can, and indeed does, vary. I will later conclude that this variation does not prevent a high correlation between total unemployment and disequilibrium unemployment. It is conceivable, however, that better measures of tightness might exist.

Indeed, there are reasons to believe that a better measure can often be found if one considers what has been called "the Beveridge curve." This curve represents the inverse correlation that can be observed between the short-term variations of the unemployment rate and of the "vacancy rate," i.e. the ratio between the number of vacant

---

[9] In stating his theory of the movements of the price level, Friedman did, however, choose a definition of the "natural unemployment rate" that refers to an equilibrium, and so to something like frictional unemployment. This rate has "the level that would be ground out by the Walrasian system of general equilibrium equations, provided there is imbedded within them the actual structural characteristics of the labor and commodity markets, including market imperfections, stochastic variability in demands and supplies, the cost of gathering information about job vacancies and labor availabilities, the costs of mobility, and so on." See M. Friedman, "The role of monetary policy," *American Economic Review* (March 1968). But no attempt was really made to directly apply this definition to any economy and, indeed, what the supposed Walrasian system of equations would be is still obscure. As an aside, we may note that this quotation, among others, shows that Friedman must be a disequilibrium economist in his explanation of actual unemployment.

jobs and the size of the labor force (see figure 3). If this curve applied exactly and never changed, the vacancy rate would provide essentially the same measure of tightness of the labor market as does the unemployment rate: a tight labor market would mean one in which unemployment is low and vacancies are numerous. But it has been observed that the Beveridge curve sometimes moves, so that the same rate of unemployment, recorded at two distinct times, may correspond to substantially different vacancy rates.[10] It is, then, difficult to say that the tightness has not changed, since firms have more unfilled standing job offers in one case than in the other. (In figure 3, the labor market seems to be tighter at point B than at point A.) A more neutral measure, which would consider on an equal basis two indicators concerning the pending supply of, and the pending demand for, labor, would be the ratio between the two rates (points A and C would then be said to correspond to the same degree of tightness).

One way to settle the issue might be to consider which measure best explains the pressure that labor market tightness puts on wages. Most econometric studies concerning changes of wage rates have followed the Phillips curve tradition in assuming that the unemployment rate was the appropriate indicator of this pressure. But a recent study on US data has concluded that the vacancy rate (as measured by the number of "help wanted" advertisements) contributes much better to explaining changes in the wage rate than does the unemployment rate.[11] On the other hand, French econometricians, who have looked rather

---

[10] Evidence showing that such shifts occurred in most countries have been gathered in OECD, "The present unemployment problem" (Working Paper CPE/WP1, June 1983).

[11] J. Medoff, "US Labor markets: Imbalance, wage growth and productivity in the 1970s," *Brookings Papers on Economic Activity* (no. 1, 1983).

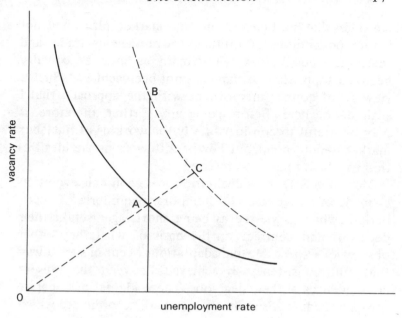

FIGURE 3　The Beveridge curve

closely at the relationship, have found that the logarithm or the ratio between vacancies and unemployment was almost always the best regressor to use in wage equations.[12]

The Working of the Labor Market

To some economists the idea that disequilibrium could be observed in a market appears paradoxical, because they

---

[12] See, in particular, D. Déruelle, "Hausse à court terme du salaire nominal, tension du marché du travail et mouvements des prix et du SMIC," *Revue Economique* (May 1975); D. Déruelle, "Détermination à court terme des hausses de salaire: études sectorielles et régionales," *Annales de l'INSEE* (December 1974). For a recent confirmation see P. Artus et al., *METRIC: Une modélisation de l'économie française* (Paris: INSEE, 1981).

consider that participants in any market place will not ignore possibilities of mutually advantageous trade, and that such possibilities will remain as long as equality between supply and demand has not been achieved. Such a view is, of course, inconsistent with the approach that I shall adopt here. Before going any further, therefore, it may be useful to consider briefly the working of the labor market and to point out how it differs from the idealization to which I have just referred.

More precisely, this idealization sees economic evolution as made of a succession of "temporary equilibria." In each period, which is viewed as being short, agents take their decisions and contract on the basis of what they either observe or expect. Mutual adaptations occur in such a way that full consistency is achieved between the present consequences of these decisions. These adaptations operate through the law of supply and demand, according to which the price of each good or service at any time is that which will clear the market for this good or service.

If, for instance, the demand for labor shifts whereas the supply does not, in any period of time in a particular region for a particular type of workers, then the wage rate paid to these workers in this region will change during this period, downward if demand decreases, upward if it increases. The change will go as far as is required for maintaining equality between supply and demand. If supply is completely rigid, employment and hours of work will not change. If this is not the case, some quantity adaptation will occur: for instance, in the case of a shift to a smaller demand for labor and, therefore, a decreased wage rate, one may expect that some workers will decide to stop working or to work fewer hours.

It is clear that the labor market does not operate in this way. Wages are not flexible in the short term in the way assumed by this form of the law of supply and demand.

They are not completely insensitive to pressure on the labor market, but they adjust much less than would be required for permanent market clearing.

For workers already employed by a company wages are usually revised periodically. Many of these revisions follow rules that have been prearranged and that make no reference to supply or demand in the market. For instance, wages are raised so as to compensate for increases in the cost of living and at longer intervals they are renegotiated. Many considerations then come into play and the pressure of demand for labor is one of them, but the rule that the new wage should be searched and selected so as to equate the demand and supply of labor is never followed.

For newly recruited workers the common understanding is that they should be paid according to the same wage scheme that already applies to other employees of the same company. The scheme may vary from one firm to another and give, for instance, more or less credit to seniority, but this does not affect the close ties between the remuneration of new employees and that of older ones. We must admit, however, that, notably in small firms and for employees with higher qualifications, a margin of wage discussion remains at the time of recruitment and pressure of demand for labor then again plays a role, but obviously not such a role as to lead to market clearing.

This description of wage determination should take into account the legislation and regulations that exist everywhere in order to protect workers against exploitation and to reduce the frequency of industrial conflicts. It should also take into account the degree of collective organization of labor and management, as well as all considerations that affect their respective powers at any time. Legislation and trade union power vary from one country to another, so that the impact of disequilibria in the labor market also varies, but is nowhere strong, except perhaps in the long term.

To conclude, let me say that the law of supply and demand is not completely inactive in the labor market, but that its influence is slow and, therefore, quite limited in the short term. Large quantity adjustments then have to occur: hours of work are changed, recruitments are accelerated or stopped, or lay-offs of greater or lesser numbers of workers decided upon.

Why is this so? Why is it that, when mass unemployment exists, unemployed workers and profit-seeking firms do not immediately arrange employment at lower wages than the prevailing ones, thus forcing the market to quickly find equilibrium? Answering the question does not seem difficult, except perhaps for economists who have acquired through their education an intellectual apparatus that they tend to apply everywhere and, therefore, sometimes in the wrong place: such behavior by firms and unemployed workers would go against social norms and would, therefore, often turn out not to be mutually advantageous.

I need not argue at length when stating that public opinion is very far from accepting the idea that the wage rate for a particular type of labor ought at any particular time to be the price that clears the corresponding labor market at that time. The accepted view is that a wage is the income earned by someone who brings his or her work to some collective activity. We also expect that this person be treated with the respect due to a human being, granted a fair degree of security of employment and income, and be protected against the risk of exploitation. Employers, therefore, consider themselves as, and are expected to be, committed to keeping their existing employees and to paying them the expected remuneration, unless compelling reasons force them not to do so.

Let us, then, consider the so-called mutually advantageous contract in which an unemployed person would

n should also be made of recent theoretical
intended to clarify why workers and employers
ree on explicit or implicit contracts in which a
al wage for a relatively long period is guaranteed,
stable employment is not. Clearly, the latter fact
y related to wage rigidity. The literature on this
n started with two articles published ten years ago
s since become very mathematical and technical.[13]
sses a double asymmetry between workers and
yers: workers are more risk-averse than employers,
ill be less well informed about the good or bad
es that their firms experience. Already, it is clear
he models being discussed will have some explanatory
r, in particular with respect to the precise content of
contracts. But it is too early to pretend that we can
firm conclusions from them in the context of these
res. Another reason for caution is that the models
deal with partial equilibria, whereas the ultimate
is to answer a question about general equilibrium.
y does incomplete market clearing result from rational
nomic behavior?[14]

different, but not conflicting, aspect of labor relations

---

[13] See M.N. Baily, "Wages and employment under uncertain
emand," *Review of Economic Studies* (January 1974); C. Azariadis,
Implicit contracts and underemployment equilibria," *Journal of
Political Economy* (December 1975). For surveys on the development of the subsequent research see O.D. Hart, "Optimal labor
contracts under asymmetric information: an introduction," *Review
of Economic Studies* (January 1983); C. Azariadis and J. Stiglitz,
"Implicit contracts and fixed-price equilibria," *Quarterly Journal
of Economics* (Supplement 1983).
[14] K. Burdett and D. Mortensen in "Search, layoffs and labor market
equilibrium," *Journal of Political Economy* (August 1980) have
discussed an equilibrium with long-term contracts in which some
workers accept attachment to the firms employing them and may
then be temporarily laid off in times of bad business conditions.

accept a job from a firm a
the going rate. In many co
to dismiss one of its existin
so such a contract may no
instance, the firm wishes t
does not face a collective wa
of new employees at wage
ones will provoke hostility fr
labor—management relations
affect the public image of the
and even, perhaps, strikes. The
much more than the saving on
most people are not moved by fi
it is in their interests not only to
feel morally right and socially r
consideration means that, for t
type of competition that is assume
of the law of supply and demand ma

Before leaving this discussion of t
are sticky, even in times of high un
add two side comments, one on me
on a recent line of related research.

In contrast to what some econom
the ability to explain an observed fact
tion for a science to take this fact int
build on it new theoretical arguments
science except mathematics, observed f
explained by other, more fundamental, c
of the logical chain there always is some u
Economics is, therefore, not at fault in c
consequences of wage rigidity if this rigi
proved to exist (see page 27). Of course, exp
are (or would be) useful for subsequent scien
but even if they are (or were) lacking, it w
wrong to overlook the observed facts.

Mentio
research
often ag
stable re
whereas
is close
questio
and ha
It stre
emplo
and v
fortur
that t
powe
labor
draw
lect
still
aim
Wh
eco

has been stressed here, namely that social norms make labor quite different from commodities. It more directly explains why some disequilibrium between supply and demand can be observed in the labor market.

Proofs of Disequilibrium Unemployment

1. Changes of Frictional Unemployment are too Small

Recognition of the logical possibility of a phenomenon is not a demonstration of its actual significance. In order to complete our understanding of mass unemployment, we must, therefore, make sure that disequilibrium in the labor market is, indeed, significant. The proposition that I have already stated, and on which we must concentrate our inquiry, is as follows: no matter what convention has been adopted for frictional unemployment, as long as this definition is sensible, disequilibrium on the labor market is proved to change through time and space.

The proof of the proposition consists of two parts. First, each of the various reasons that were suggested as causing changes of frictional unemployment can only account for small changes. Even taken together, these reasons can only explain a small part of the actual changes in unemployment. They cannot fully explain its large fluctuations in North America, nor its current trend in Western Europe. Second, the hypothesis of a changing disequilibrium in the labor market has a much better explanatory power for a number of observed facts than the alternative hypothesis of labor-market clearing.

Changes of frictional unemployment may come from voluntary changes of the mean time spent by individuals in their search for a job. It is, indeed, conceivable that, given that the pressure of labor demand on labor supply remains the same, unemployed people might spend either more or less time before accepting a job. This change in behavior might occur either because of a change in the composition of the labor force or because of a change in the economic conditions faced by the unemployed.

As for the changing structure of the labor force, we could on occasion in the late sixties and in the seventies point to the effect of the increasing proportion of women and young workers who spend on average more time in their search for a job than do adult men. But it can easily be seen that such shifts only explain a quite small and slow change of aggregate unemployment.[15]

More interesting is the study of the possible impact of better compensation for loss of resources because of unemployment. Search theory has shown that, not surprisingly, the optimal search time increases with the reservation wage (the wage at which a worker decides to accept the first offer of employment) and that better compensation for unemployment leads to a higher reservation wage.[16] Since this compensation increased in most Western countries in the sixties or seventies, it is relevant to turn to econometric studies for an evaluation of its effect.

This has been the subject of a number of papers in the USA, a survey of which has been given by D. Hamermesh.[17]

---

[15] See, for instance, R.T. Kaufman, "Patterns of unemployment in North America, Western Europe and Japan," in Malinvaud and Fitoussi (eds), *Unemployment in Western Countries*.

[16] For a neat presentation of the mathematics of search theory and of its application to the labor market, see S.A. Lippman and J.J. MacCall, "The economics of job search: a survey," *Economic Inquiry* (June and September 1976).

[17] D. Hamermesh, *Jobless Pay and the Economy* (Baltimore: Johns Hopkins University Press, 1977). The result of a very extensive recent study of the USA may also be mentioned here. Considering the extreme hypothesis of a complete elimination of unemployment

The general conclusion is that better unemployment compensation did indeed induce some increases in job-search time, but that the scale and timing of this effect remained limited. Econometric work in Western Europe leads to the same conclusions. For instance, S.J. Nickell estimates that unemployment in the UK increased by 13 per cent between 1964–5 and 1973 as a result of a better compensation for loss of income, but measured unemployment increased by 92 per cent during the same period and kept increasing later on, whereas compensation no longer improved.[18]

Changes of frictional unemployment may also come from a varying degree of mismatch between the composition of labor supply and that of labor demand.[19] This mismatch has many dimensions. Two of them seem to have been particularly considered: the first concerns the professional and geographical composition of the labor force and the second draws attention to the low-qualification, low-ability sector of the population.

The professional and geographical structure of labor supply has experienced sustained shifts. By and large, this

---

insurance, the authors deduce from their estimates that the 1978 unemployment rate would have decreased as a result from 6.00 to 5.35 per cent. A more acceptable 10 per cent reduction in unemployment insurance benefits would have resulted in an unemployment rate of 5.92 per cent. See K.B. Clark and L.H. Summers, "Unemployment insurance and labor market transitions," in M.N. Baily (ed.), *Workers, Jobs and Inflation* (Washington: Brookings Institution, 1982).

[18] S.J. Nickell, "The effect of unemployment and related benefit on the duration of unemployment", *Economic Journal* (March 1979).

[19] Recognizing the existence of such a mismatch is admitting that market clearing does not occur completely at the micro-level. That the market-clearing hypothesis could be kept at the macro-level in such a situation may seem somewhat odd. We shall come back on this point in the next section.

long-term movement has been consistent with the simultaneous shift in the composition of labor demand. But consistency does not apply to short-term changes. Business fluctuations, as well as sudden shocks of a different nature, generate changes in the demands coming from various industries and, therefore, also in the composition of labor demand by professions and geographical areas. When these changes are particularly rapid, it is natural that frictional unemployment increases.

A few econometric studies have attempted to grasp the effect of this factor. Reference may here be made to a recent study for the USA by D.M. Lilien.[20] The author considers the standard deviation, between manufacturing industries, of a variable that measures the yearly need for recruitment (if positive) or lay-off (if negative). He then shows that this variable explains part of the fluctuations in the unemployment rate, peaks of unemployment in 1954, 1958, 1971 and 1975 being associated with particularly high interindustrial dispersion of changes in labor demand. (The specification of the regression may, however, tend to overestimate this effect since, except for the dispersion variable, it contains only a time trend and an indicator of the so-called unanticipated monetary policy as regressors, but no variable directly related to autonomous demand for goods or to other determinants of the demand for labor.)

Employment of poorly qualified workers may be made more difficult by legislation or practices intended to protect labor. In particular, imposition of a minimum wage could push out of employment workers whose productivity would be lower than this minimum, if their productivity could be exactly measured. We might, therefore, postulate that frictional unemployment increases when the ratio

---

[20] D.M. Lilien, "Sectoral shifts and cyclical unemployment," *Journal of Political Economy* (August 1982).

between the legal minimum and the current mean wage increases.

This relationship has been the object of a large number of econometric studies that have been recently surveyed.[21] The general conclusion is that a high minimum wage does induce a significant increase in youth unemployment, but that no significant impact appears for adult men or women workers. Since the large fluctuations of unemployment affect all kinds of workers, minimum wage legislation can only explain a very small part of the general phenomenon.

We have just looked at four different factors that might explain changes of frictional unemployment. Each one of these is valid in itself but can only explain a small part of the actual changes in recorded unemployment. Even taking the effect of all four together does not invalidate this conclusion. In France, for instance, unemployment multiplied by ten, from 200,000 in 1962 to 2 million in 1982. We can venture to say that our four factors only raised frictional unemployment by between 200,000 and 500,000. This is, admittedly, only a "guesstimate," but it conveys a correct view of the disproportion between what has to be explained and what may be explained by frictional unemployment.

2. *Permanent Market Clearing is an Untenable Hypothesis*

Instead of focusing attention on frictional unemployment, we may look at mass unemployment from a different angle and wonder which one of two hypotheses, disequilibrium

---

[21] C. Brown, C. Gilroy and A. Kohen, "The effect of minimum wage on employment and unemployment," *Journal of Economic Literature* (June 1982). Analysis of French data tends to support the conclusions of this article. See, in particular, John P. Martin, "Effect of minimum wage on the youth labor market in North America and France," OECD *Occasional Studies* (June 1983).

or market-clearing, best fits the facts. For this discussion we may start from a very simple formalization, which will help to organize our thoughts.

Let labor supply and demand be L^s and L^d respectively, the real wage rate be w and the autonomous determinants of supply and demand be z^s and z^d. Then

$$L^s = aw + z^s \tag{1}$$

$$L^d = -bw + z^d \tag{2}$$

a and b being two numerical coefficients. The market-clearing hypothesis requires $L^s = L^d$; hence the real wage rate must adjust:

$$w = \frac{z^d - z^s}{a + b} \qquad L = \frac{az^d + bz^s}{a + b} \tag{3}$$

Doubts about the realism of this hypothesis stem from the feeling that it would require a much larger variability of real wages than is observed. Indeed, suppose that z^s and z^d independently fluctuate around their trend values with variances σ_s^2 and σ_d^2. The real wage rate and employment fluctuate with variances that are related by:

$$\frac{\text{Var}(w)}{\text{Var}(L)} = \frac{\sigma_d^2 + \sigma_s^2}{a^2 \sigma_d^2 + b^2 \sigma_s^2} \tag{4}$$

Moreover, the prevailing view is that the labor supply is quite rigid, so that a and σ_s^2/σ_d^2 are small. The observed sluggishness of the real wage rate together with the observed variability of employment seem to be inconsistent with the required equality (4). On the other hand, the observed inverse correlation between variations of unemployment and variations of employment fits well with the notion of a rigid labor supply, a rigid real wage rate and an important disequilibrium component $L^s - L^d$ of unemployment.

To get an idea of the variability of the market-clearing wage rate that may follow from models of temporary equilibria applied to quarterly macroeconomic data, we may consider figure 4, taken from an econometric study of the French economy.[22] The aim was to determine what should have been the real wage rate if the two markets for goods and labor had to be cleared in a given quarter, notwithstanding the shocks that occurred in this quarter. The calculation used the structural equations of a fitted macroeconometric model. The shock occurring in a quarter was not exactly known, but its probability distribution could

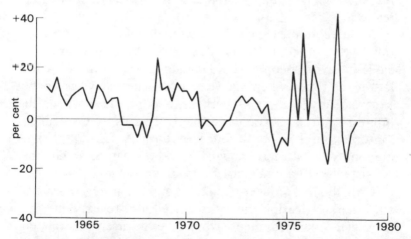

FIGURE 4 The percentage difference between the competitive equilibrium and observed real wage rates in France

---

[22] P. Artus, G. Laroque and G. Michel, "Estimation of a quarterly macroeconomic model with quantity rationing," forthcoming in *Econometrica*.

be estimated from the model and from the values taken by the observed variables during this quarter. Hence, the expected value of the market clearing real wage could be computed. Figure 4 plots the series of the difference between this expected value and the actual wage rate. We can see that the difference fluctuates widely and that at times exceeds 20 per cent.

Of course, this result depends strongly on the whole specification of the model, which is assumed to be the appropriate representation of French macroeconomic evolution. This is not the place to discuss this specification and to examine which important features it may overlook, but we should note that the labor supply is assumed to be almost completely rigid. According to the few equations given above, this may be partly responsible for the high variability of the computed market-clearing real wage.

Some economists have presented arguments as to why the labor supply might be flexible.[23] According to a life cycle behavior, people would decide to substitute work for leisure at times when they consider the real wage to be exceptionally high, and perhaps also at times when the interest rate is particularly high. This is the so-called "intertemporal substitution hypothesis." If the phenomenon were strong enough, market clearing might be consistent with a small variability of real wages.

Actually, in order to make the facts fully consistent with market-clearing theory, we need also to explain why frictional unemployment would be inversely correlated with employment. This is sometimes done by saying that a high real wage is also higher than that anticipated by job

---

[23] R.E. Lucas Jr and L. Rapping, "Real wages, employment and inflation," *Journal of Political Economy* (1969).

seekers, so that a short time is needed for them to find a wage offer exceeding their reservation wage. But we must then realize that this is more likely to play a significant role if real wages fluctuate substantially.

The rather small observed variability of real wages can hardly be made consistent with the market-clearing hypothesis unless there is both a large intertemporal substitution effect in labour supply and a large effect on frictional unemployment of small differences between the reservation wage and the actual wage. The simultaneous occurrence of these two properties is not likely.

Indeed, an attempt was made to fit an econometric model to the US labor market for the years 1929–76, which incorporated the substitution effect and the market-clearing hypothesis. This led to a serious questioning of the adequacy of the model.[24] It has even been argued, rather convincingly, that the intertemporal substitution property taken alone does not hold. Contrary to this property, people who have once decided to participate in the labor force tend to persist in this behavior, even after the economic motivation for it has disappeared.[25] Moreover, one should not look at the phenomenon by considering it only at the aggregate level. Market clearing appears still more far-fetched and becomes still more unlikely when one takes all dimensions into account.

First, one must take note that employment and unemployment fluctuations are particularly important for workers with low qualifications. They are precisely the

[24] See J. Altonji and O. Ashenfelter, "Wage movements and the labor market equilibrium hypothesis," *Economica* (August 1980); J. Altonji, "The intertemporal substitution model of labor market fluctuations: an empirical analysis," *Review of Economic Studies* 49 (1982).

[25] K.B. Clark and L.H. Summers, "Labor force participation: timing and persistence", *Review of Economic Studies* 49 (1982).

people who are not likely to wish at times to substitute
work for leisure and at other times leisure for work.
Second, one must realize that the market-clearing hypothesis would require that relative wages continuously
change in reaction to changes in the composition of the
demand for labor, between regions, industries and qualifications. But it is a well-known fact that workers are more
concerned with their relative wages than with their actual
wages and that, as a result, relative wages are sticky. New
local disequilibria between supply and demand for labor
then continuously appear and remain for some time:[26] this
is one good reason that frictional unemployment is
important.

At this point, reference may also be made to research
devoted to the proof of a rather strong proposition,
namely that "individual behavior is better explained when
one introduces the hypothesis that labour supply may face
a demand constraint than when one does not." It is a
stronger proposition than the one stated above (page 23)
because, if proved, it would not rely on any convention
but on information about individual behavior in order to
establish that the disequilibrium hypothesis is useful for
understanding what is happening in the labor market.

The difficulty with the proof of this proposition is the
need for a convincing framework in which individual
behavior could be tested. O. Ashenfelter, however, has
argued for econometric research based on this proposition
and reports on two studies, one of an aggregate time-
series for the USA, the other of a sample of American

---

[26] This has been shown in particular for industries in the UK by
C.A. Pissarides, "The role of relative wages and excess demand in the
sectoral flow of labour," *Review of Economic Studies* (October
1978).

individuals.[27] Both studies conclude that a large part of unemployment is involuntary. Indeed, it has been found that, if the usual determinants of labor supply are held constant, measured unemployment is negatively correlated with actual hours of work. The crucial question is, of course, to know whether all significant determinants of labor supply have been controlled in such tests. Considering the importance of the issue, these studies deserve much wider discussion and repetition than they seem so far to have stimulated.

Finally, we should not leave this question without mentioning that the disequilibrium hypothesis explains a number of observed facts about the operation of the labor market, in particular about the length of spells of unemployment. It should be observed that many of these spells of unemployment are too long to result from the voluntary behavior of job seekers. The economic conditions facing those who do not find a job quickly in the USA have been studied by K.B. Clark and L.H. Summers who, after also considering other evidence, concluded that unemployment is in large part due to incomplete market adjustment.[28]

This conclusion fits very well with another observation, namely that changes in the aggregate demand for labor, or still better, changes in its industrial and non-industrial components, are very helpful in explaining changes in the

---

[27] O. Ashenfelter, "Unemployment as a constraint of labor market behavior," in OECD, *Structural determinants of employment and unemployment* (Paris, 1979) vol. 2; O. Ashenfelter, "Unemployment as disequilibrium in a model of aggregate labor supply," *Econometrica* (April 1980).

[28] Clark and Summers, *Brookings Papers on Economic Activity* (1979); and "Unemployment reconsidered: the real problem is concentrated, long-term joblessness," *Harvard Business Review* (November–December 1980).

probability of people leaving unemployment, whether this probability is considered for all the unemployed or for subgroups that can be defined by age, sex, race, qualifications and so on.[29]

At a less specific level, we must also note that the forecasting performance of the macroeconometric models in current use is valuable, at least for the following one or two years. They are certainly not perfect, but they perform better than alternative methods of forecasting. In particular, they have been reliable in their assessment of future unemployment trends (see note 27 on page 111). Since they always deal with unemployment as a disequilibrium between the supply of, and the demand for, labor, we may take their systematic use in many countries during the past twenty years as providing us with a very serious proof that the disequilibrium hypothesis is the correct one to make.

---

[29] See, in particular, Salais, *Economie et Statistique* (1980).

2 Macroeconomic Analysis

An analytical framework is needed for the discussion of macroeconomic policies intended to curb mass unemployment. It must start from the main features of the phenomenon, namely that mass unemployment is a disequilibrium, revealing an excess supply of labor. Such a framework was provided for many years by the prevailing modelization of Keynesian theory. Recent reconsideration has, however, shown that this model is subject to many limitations, some of which now appear to be particularly serious. A fresh assessment is, therefore, required.

It appears today, much more than twenty years ago, that macroeconomic policies must be viewed in a dynamic setting, because their consequences evolve and extend far beyond the time at which they are introduced. The usual model of Keynesian theory is, however, static. Much attention must, therefore, now be devoted to studying how a dynamic analysis of mass unemployment should proceed. After a section dealing with the static analysis, the rest of this lecture will consider how the evolution of mass unemployment can be studied.

It must be said from the start that my discussion of this essential dynamic analysis will remain tentative. Economic theory does not yet provide the kind of solid framework which we should like. Thus, we shall have to satisfy ourselves with a survey of the various aspects that must be examined, and with the consideration of some preliminary attempts at building models whose various elements can deal with as many of these aspects as possible.

Short-Term Analysis

1. Keynesian theory asserts that the excess supply of labor is due to a potential excess supply of goods: firms would use more labor if they were facing a larger demand for their output, because they would then find it profitable to produce more.[1] If this is the case, the analysis of unemployment boils down to an analysis of the formation of the demand for goods. The multiplier model is the simplest framework provided for this analysis; more elaborate well-known theoretical or macroeconometric models start from the same basic principle.

Of course, Keynesian theory does not assert that excess supply of labor always holds. There may be full employment typically with an excess demand for labor, firms being then unable, because of a shortage of labor, to satisfy the full demand for their goods. A second situation may then occur, besides the one in which there is excess supply on both the labor and the goods markets: this is where there is excess demand on both markets. It is noteworthy, however, but of secondary importance for our present discussion, that no precise model of this second

---

[1] This sentence describes a situation that will be said to be "excess supply of goods." The fact that it sometimes occurs will be taken for granted here, without further discussion. But, in the same way as disequilibrium on the labor market was discussed in the preceding lecture, it would be possible and interesting to examine precisely what disequilibrium on the goods market means, why it may appear and what are the proofs of its frequent occurrence.

situation was offered by Keynesian theory, as if a static analysis of a situation of generalized excess demand were not really interesting.

The main point on which we must focus attention here is that the simultaneous occurrence of excess supply of labor and excess demand for goods was until recently not recognized as a possibility. However, reconsideration of Keynesian theory and reconstruction of its multiplier model within a more fundamental fixed-price formulation has shown that this simultaneous occurrence was at least a logical possibility. This is brought out clearly, for instance, by the now familiar Barro—Grossman model. Unemployment could exist simultaneously with excess demand for goods if, notwithstanding this excess demand, firms were unable, or did not find it profitable, to increase the scale of their operation, i.e. to produce a larger output and employ more labor.

If such a situation could occur, it would imply a quite different diagnosis from the one that is appropriate for the case of generalized excess supply. Stimulation of the demand for goods would not directly act on unemployment and measures intended to increase business profitability would be favored, inducing firms to expand their operations. Considering the stands taken by various economists within the debates that took place in the thirties, we may refer to this case as one of classical unemployment and contrast it to the more familiar one of Keynesian unemployment.

Inquiry about the role of classical unemployment follows not only from the natural development of theoretical reflection, but also from the now-frequent concern of policy makers with the restoration of profitability. This is why, at least in Western Europe, there is a great eagerness to know whether classical unemployment is more than a purely theoretical possibility.

2. One can think of two reasons that, at first sight, seem to make classical unemployment unlikely. The first stresses a supposed asymmetry in the dynamics of prices. If prices were fully and instantaneously flexible upward while remaining sticky downward, excess demand would never be observed; market disequilibria could only come from excess supplies; unemployment would be Keynesian, but not classical. Clearly, the full upward flexibility of all prices is not a realistic hypothesis to make for modern economies. But the fact remains that, if prices are more flexible upward than downward, a *prima facie* argument exists for suggesting that Keynesian unemployment is more likely than classical unemployment. In order to provide a rigorous proof of this proposition of a higher probability of Keynesian than classical unemployment, the argument should of course be imbedded in a dynamic theory; but at this stage it already offers a hint that the proposition should be true.

On the other hand, thinking of a short-term macro-economic analysis of unemployment, we must, of course, consider the current decisions of firms facing an excess demand for their output while disposing of their pre-existing equipment. The common situation is one in which the physical capacity of this equipment is not saturated. For firms to turn down the opportunity of producing and selling more, their profitability must then be quite low. Indeed, the price of output must be lower than the variable cost of one extra unit of production. This looks like an infrequent situation, since, in the long run, the price must cover both variable and fixed costs.

But an unlikely situation could, of course, occur so it becomes a question of fact whether it does or not. We can turn to econometrics for the answer but, before proceeding to econometric estimation or testing, we must set up a mathematical model that can be taken as a good first approximation of the actual working of the economy. For reasons that I shall give in a moment, we cannot consider that the Barro–Grossman model, or any similarly aggregated one, provides such a first approximation. We must, therefore, while retaining our concern for econometric tests, wait until a realistic specification is available before we can implement them.

Considering the second reason that makes classical unemployment unlikely, we realize the limitations of a purely static analysis. The pre-existing equipment depends on previous capacity building, which is related to the then-perceived profitability. After a prolonged period of low profitability, the productive capacity may be reduced in such a way as to make the variable cost of a marginal unit of output fairly high, even for a modest level of production. In other words, classical unemployment is likely to increase with time when profitability is low. The force of this reason cannot, however, be evaluated except within a dynamic formulation.

3. Even for a short-term analysis, however, it is somewhat misleading to concentrate attention on the two opposite situations of classical and Keynesian unemployment. This would only be appropriate in a world of two homogenous markets: *the* market for labor and *the* market for goods. There are, however, many types of labor, many different goods and, for most types of labor and kinds of goods, several geographical areas to consider, to the extent that supply and demand are specific to one or other of these areas. This means that there are a large number of distinct markets with as many potential disequilibria characterized by either excess supply or excess demand. Keynesian and classical unemployment could be considered as resulting only from two extreme cases, all labor markets being in excess supply in both cases, with all goods markets being

simultaneously in excess supply for the Keynesian case, and in excess demand for the classical one.

A realistic theory must recognize the existence of a wide two-dimensional spectrum of situations in between the three extreme ones: excess supplies everywhere, excess demands everywhere, and excess supplies for all types of labor simultaneously with excess demands for all kinds of goods. These three polar situations correspond respectively to full Keynesian unemployment, full latent inflation, and full classical unemployment. The fourth polar situation is usually not given much attention, because we admit that firms cannot be simultaneously subject to two bounding constraints — lack of labor and lack of demand. Excess demand for labor by a firm therefore implies in practice excess demand for its product; generalized excess demand for labor cannot coexist with generalized excess supply of goods (we shall keep to this admittedly simplified hypothesis, but it plays no crucial role).

The multiplicity of feasible situations within a spectrum spanned by these three would make any kind of analysis untractable if we could not treat it from a statistical viewpoint. Quite naturally, we are led to wonder how we could deal with the problems while thinking in terms of amount of Keynesian unemployment and amount of classical unemployment. We shall be able to do so rather easily if we can couple labor markets with goods markets, so that we define sectors consisting of a labor market and a goods market. Each sector can then be said to be in a Keynesian, inflationary or classical situation, depending on the combination of excess demands or supplies that it experiences. The relative weight of the sectors that are in the Keynesian situation can be taken as the appropriate measure for the amount of Keynesian unemployment.

Defining sectors by coupling a labor market and a goods market necessarily implies some simplification. Even so, it probably cannot be properly done unless some labor markets are put in two or more sectors, and some goods markets as well. For instance, one sector might consist of skilled labor in the middle-west mechanical industry, another one of unskilled labor in the same industry, even though the unskilled labor supply may in fact not be specific to this industry. This example shows the type of simplification that is involved. Dealing with the situation in the first sector we neglect the possibility that the industry might be bound by a constraint on unskilled labor; in other words, we neglect the fact that the goods supply must be the same in the two sectors. On the other hand, we may be led to underestimate the mobility of un-skilled labor from this industry to another one in the same region.

I do not mean that dealing with sectors, in the way I am suggesting, is necessary for a macroeconomic analysis adopting a statistical viewpoint but, rather, that it makes such an analysis easier than it would otherwise be, and that I accept the simplification at present, while recognizing its limitations. The specification of a theoretical model adopting such a sectoral framework should permit us to study the macroeconomic equilibrium and how it reacts to changes of policy variables. It will then serve the same function as does the multiplier model or the Barro–Grossman model but it will be more realistic in its recognition of the multiplicity of goods and types of labor.

The definition of sectors is not enough to determine a model describing short-term equilibrium. We also need to specify a number of other elements. Simplicity, then, has a large premium. With this in mind, we may admit that a few macroeconomic variables are enough to characterize the state of the economy. For instance, the price of the various goods will be directly tied to a single variable p, the price level, and the wages rates of the various types of labor will be similarly tied to a single representative wage rate w. The supply of labor in each sector and the demand for the output of each sector may also be assumed to depend on a few variables applying to the whole economy, such as the real wage rate, the government aggregate demand and the aggregate income of all individuals. Finally, simple assumptions, such as fixed input—output coefficients, may be made in order to determine the supply of output and the demand for labor in each sector.

Following such principles I have been able to specify a rather simple multisectoral model and to derive a number of theoretical results from it.[2] Clearly, these results depend on the particular assumptions I have chosen; they have not been discussed enough for their strength to be assessed at present. But I feel confident about the following qualitative conclusions: the multiplier defining the sensitivity of aggregate output with respect to government demand, which has its traditional expression when the economy is in the state of full Keynesian unemployment, rather quickly decreases when the extent of such unemployment decreases. More generally, when the number of sectors is large, non-linear but smooth relations appear to link endogenous variables to exogenous ones. The partial derivative of one endogenous variable, such as the

---

[2] The model was first presented in my paper "Rationing of employment," in Malinvaud and Fitoussi (eds), *Unemployment in Western Countries*.

An improved presentation of a variant of the model appears in the French version of the paper, published in my *Essais sur la théorie du chômage* (Paris: Calmann-Lévy, 1983). The same idea of specifying a statistical distribution of market disequilibria was used by J. Muellbauer and D. Winter, "Unemployment, employment and exports in British manufacturing: a non-clearing markets approach," *European Economic Review* (May 1980).

unemployment rate, with respect to one exogenous variable, such as the wage rate, may change sign when the economy moves from one state to another. It may be negative when unemployment is predominantly Keynesian but positive when it is predominantly classical.

4. In order to improve the process of short-term macroeconomic analysis, we should not only elaborate theoretical models that permit an abstract discussion of the properties of the phenomena, but should also carefully examine the econometric transposition of these models. It is far from being always true that a pure application of a good theoretical model provides a good econometric specification, or even a good framework for less-formal applied analysis. The abstractions embodied in a theoretical model may be convenient for the careful scrutiny of a particular relationship but they may, nevertheless, be quite inappropriate for the representation of the actual economy.

Considering how important the new developments in the macroeconomic theory of unemployment have been during the recent years, it is clear that their implications for applied work ought to be extensively discussed. Such a discussion has, indeed, started but is still at a preliminary stage and requires much more attention than has so far been given to it. I can, of course, not claim to complete it here; I have not even the time to explain what my ideas about it are at present.[3] I shall, therefore, limit myself here to making just one general comment.

The revision of our present practice in econometric or applied work should concentrate on developing appropriate non-linear models within which variables describing the

---

[3] I have tried to proceed to a more thorough discussion in "Analyse macroéconomique des déséquilibres: la France des vingt dernières années," in *Essais sur la théorie du chômage.*

direction and intensity of disequilibria could be assigned
their correct role. The pure transposition of models such
as the Barro–Grossman one is not the best solution, even
though experimenting with this transposition does present
some interest for research workers, and for me in
particular. The best solution is probably much closer to
the one chosen already long ago by some econometric
model builders who had the intuitive feeling that non-
linearities and variables measuring disequilibria were
important. What is now needed is to provide a stronger
foundation to this intuition and to develop a methodology
in order to rigorously and correctly take it into account in
our work.

Three Sources of Spontaneous Evolution

An analysis of economies experiencing disequilibria such as
mass unemployment cannot be purely static. For one
thing, speaking of a disequilibrium itself suggests that the
situation will move. Reference to the common meaning of
disequilibrium should, of course, not be given too much
weight in our thinking since disequilibrium has here a
different meaning, namely the existence of excess supply
or demand, but economists also admit that such im-
balances between supply and demand stimulate corrective
changes. Moreover, the present concern about economic
policies no longer stresses their short-term impact, but
rather questions how policies will contribute to improving
the situation in the medium or even the long term. Dealing
with the longer lasting impact of policy measures requires
reflection on models that take the forces of economic
evolution into account; it requires consideration of truly
dynamic models.

    An economist endowed with a classical training and

thinking about disequilibria between supply and demand naturally turns his attention towards price movements, but we must recognize that other dynamic changes also play an important role. I am even ready to argue that, for the macroeconomic analysis of modern economies, these other dynamic changes should often play a larger part than price changes. In any case, we must consider them carefully.

For my survey of the dynamic forces that we must take into account, it is convenient to think of three main sources of spontaneous economic evolution: changes of price aggregates, capital accumulation and microeconomic

competition among to lower their price normally lower the increase. Similarly, wn the evolution of should push it up. ate and of the price intensity of the dis- arkets respectively. rice aggregates was 1, it played a large he sustainability of it of econometrics day, however, with t we know about it found to exist but it may at times be wages and prices, ie and space with

conometric work is the Phillips curve,

relating the rate of increase of the nominal wage rate to the rate of unemployment, gave a very simple form and were good. The relation already appeared to be non-linear, the sensitivity of wages to high levels of unemployment being weak. Experience in the late sixties and the seventies showed that, in order to have a good fit, we should pay attention to a correct specification of the impact of the past evolution of the price level, recognize the role of exogenous factors such as the legal regulation of the minimum wage or raw material price shocks deteriorating business profits, and admit that the relation changes through time and space. In particular, it has been found that reactions of the wage rate to unemployment are now weaker than they were during the first part of this century and that in some European countries changes of consumer prices are fully and very quickly transmitted to wages, so that disequilibrium on the labor market should be seen there as reacting to the speed of variation of the real wage rate.[4]

In any case, a correct representation of the dynamic process relating changes of the wage rate and the price level to macroeconomic disequilibria must take the strong relationship between wages and prices into account. The direct effect of disequilibrium on the goods market must then be correctly identified. It has been found to be weak, and some economists have even claimed that the price level adapted according to a cost-plus relationship. The

---

[4] Concerning the historical comparison see, for France, R. Boyer, "Les salaires en longue période," *Economie et Statistique* (September 1978) and, for the USA, J. Sachs, "The changing cyclical behavior of wages and prices: 1890–1976," *American Economic Review* (March 1980). For international comparisons see P. Artus, "Formation conjointe des prix et des salaires dans cinq grands pays industriels: peut-on comprendre les écarts entre les taux d'inflation?" *Annales de l'INSEE* (January–March 1983).

evidence seems now to show that this was too extreme a view and that pressure of demand on the goods market plays some independent part in accelerating the inflationary process, independently of the wage push stimulated by the pressure that most often also appears on the labor market when excess demand for goods occurs.

No matter how we look at the econometric evidence, we must reach the conclusion that the law of supply and demand acts rather slowly at the macroeconomic level we are considering. This may call for some theoretical explanation and has indeed stimulated reflection by a number of economists. I dealt with the question myself for the labor market in my first lecture (see pages 17–23); somewhat similar considerations have been applied to the goods market. The main purpose here must be to study the consequences of this observation.

2. One clear consequence is that the speed of price and wage adjustments does not have a different order of magnitude than the speed of capital accumulation and that, in any complete macroeconomic dynamic model, both processes must be considered simultaneously. Unfortunately, our ideas about capital accumulation are rather vague and we can claim no precision for the way in which we deal with it in our macroeconomic analyses.

Present private savings are important for future aggregate demand because they increase private wealth and because greater wealth implies a higher demand for consumption. The relationship seems to be quite simple. However, we have not mastered it. The main reason for this may be the lack of data on which to test our ideas and to use in our applied work. Whereas national income and product accounts are now available for a substantial period in all developed countries, related national balance sheets are not computed, except on very rare occasions. This explains in particular why the propensity to spend out of wealth is not precisely known.

The difficulties faced by statisticians proving themselves unable to regularly produce national balance sheets may, however, come from the fact that the dynamic link between saving and wealth is not that simple both because of permanent changes in capital valuation where it occurs and lack of capital valuation in many instances. Real capital gains and losses are often important and should not be neglected in applied or even theoretical work. We should distinguish perceived gains and losses from unperceived ones, and anticipated ones from the unanticipated.

We cannot say that the econometrics of investment has been neglected, considering how many contributions have been devoted to it. Since many factors act on investment, it is natural to record that, unfortunately, the impact of some of them is not precisely measured. But we can be satisfied that the most important factor, the accelerator phenomenon, has been well identified. From our point of view these econometric results are, nevertheless, deficient in one important respect. A dynamic disequilibrium analysis requires that attention be given to some features that have not been much studied. This applies particularly when we want to diagnose whether something like classical unemployment occurs.

The excess demand for goods that characterizes classical unemployment in theoretical models usually corresponds in reality to a lack of productive capacity because of insufficient capacity building or untimely scrapping. Our present concern for classical unemployment comes, indeed, from the fact that a lack of productive capacity is quite real now in many areas of the industrial world and makes mass unemployment unavoidable there, at least in the short term. But it is not common either in theoretical or econometric works, to distinguish between the two dimensions of capital and the two corresponding types of investment: capital deepening and capital widening.

Low capacity building or early scrapping is often attributed to low profitability. It is then argued that the profits that can be earned by operating the relevant capacity are expected to be small, perhaps even negative. But this concept of profitability has not been given much consideration in econometric work, except by James Tobin with his q ratio, which I should prefer, however, not to be necessarily measured from stock market valuations.[5]

These considerations explain why I have recently concentrated my attention on specifications stressing these two neglected dimensions: productive capacity and profitability. As is the case with the putty-clay technology, the capital stock has both a productive capacity, and a capital intensity, i.e. a labor requirement by unit of output. My thesis states that the main factors explaining changes of capacity are the accelerator and business profitability, or equivalently Tobin's q. On the other hand, the main factor explaining changes in labor requirement is the relative cost of capital with respect to labor.[6]

Clearly, profitability must be understood as a measure of a disequilibrium existing in the price system, the same being true of Tobin's q. It may be defined, for instance, as the pure profit rate, namely the excess of the real profit

---

[5] For a fuller discussion about the state of the econometrics of investment seen from this viewpoint, see E. Malinvaud, "La profitabilité comme facteur de l'investissement," *Rheinisch–Westfälische Akademie der Wissenschaften, Vorträge* N 310 (Westdeutscher Verlag, 1982).

[6] The rationale for this thesis has been presented in various forms in some of my writings. Its best presentation probably is E. Malinvaud, "Profitability and investment facing uncertain demand" (Paris: INSEE, 1983).

rate earned on productive operations over the real interest rate earned on finance capital. The frequent existence of such disequilibria in the price system is an observed fact.[7] This is not surprising as soon as one perceives that at the macroeconomic level, the law of supply and demand acts slowly and is sometimes dominated by price or wage shocks.

If I am speaking of "my thesis" it is because I strongly believe it to be true, but also because I have, for the time being, no proof that it is widely accepted. I hasten to add that, even if my thesis is true, the econometric estimates that would measure the various coefficients involved in its formulation are still lacking.

3. Mass unemployment is the result of many distinct situations at the micro level and of many microdecisions. While it is related to the macroeconomic trends, it also depends on more localized factors and on how agents confronted with them react. Even a macroeconomic analysis should not neglect this extra dimension of the phenomenon. In particular, the dynamic analysis of unemployment, which considers why adjustments are not quicker or more satisfactorily oriented, must pay some attention to mobility of labor and capital from contracting to expanding activities.

That it should be so is quite natural since mass unemployment is a disequilibrium. Its existence comes from the fact that, because the law of supply and demand ruling price changes is sluggish, quantities have to adapt. But by how much one particular quantity, the aggregate excess

---

[7] For instance, in France, the pure profit rate may be estimated to have decreased by 7 per cent on an annual basis, between the early 1970s and 1982. (See Malinvaud, *Essais*.)

supply of labor, has to adapt depends on how sluggish is the adaptation of other quantities.

I argued earlier that the proper vision of the macro-economic state was to see it as resulting from a wide variety of microeconomic disequilibria. While some sectors experience excess supply, others are in a situation of excess demand. A good deal of these disequilibria can be reabsorbed by the intersectoral mobility of supply and demand, people moving, for instance, from areas or industries where vacant jobs are lacking to those where they exist. If, for some reason, behavior changes so that this mobility is reduced, the consequence should be a higher unemployment than it would otherwise be.

It has often been argued that this aspect of the pheno-menon is as important as the sluggishness of the law of supply and demand and the vagaries of capital accumula-tion. But in most macroeconomic analyses of unemploy-ment it is actually neglected. One good reason may be that changes of behavior with respect to mobility were assumed to be slow, but since macroeconomic analyis now turns its attention to the longer term, this no longer holds. Another reason may simply be that our knowledge of mobility behavior is scanty. Indeed, the subject is probably not one on which economists feel particularly at home. It requires a good grasp of the institutional context, and it involves psychosociology. This is, however, no good reason for forgetting about it.

Statistical data on mobility do exist. Its changes through space and time can be described with an accuracy that is certainly not perfect but that compares with that achieved for many other subjects of economic statistics. What is so described is, however, not the fundamental behavior but rather its result while it operates in a changing environ-ment. Models are then required for the estimation of behavior shifts that observed evolution may reveal. For instance, observed labor mobility increased in France during the sixties and is usually attributed not to changes in behavior, but to the presence of new attractive jobs created by a boom of industrial investment. Or, again, labor mobility has to be low in a country in which unemployment prevails in all regions and all industries.

Mobility behavior is, of course, one aspect of job search. The same factors that explain why search activities become more or less intensive may also explain a higher or lower mobility. Or the factors that lead those who are looking for jobs to decrease their reservation wage may also make them more willing to move. But some factors may also affect mobility without touching other aspects of search. It is easy, then, to imagine a wide range of research that would be useful but, so far as I know, the econometrics of mobility behavior is not yet very advanced and has basically only shown that the phenomenon is quite complex.[8]

It is sometimes argued that European economies experience a rigidity that prevents many types of adjustments, including those that would be permitted by greater worker mobility. The present extent of unemployment in Western Europe could be partly due to this. The suggestion does not seem to have been the object of rigorous scrutiny but it has some force. Rigidity refers not only to the behavior of workers looking for jobs, but also to the management of the labor force within companies. It may be due to legal or other institutional changes making layoffs more difficult and inducing, as a consequence, more cautious recruitment.

Precisely because of the presence of disequilibria and

---

[8] See, in particular, Ehrenberg and Smith, *Modern Labor Economics*, chapter 10; and M.J. Greenwood, "Research on Internal Migration in the United States: A Survey," *Journal of Economic Literature* (June 1975).

because of the rigidity within the existing economy, however, society finds new ways of partially adapting itself. Some unemployed people are offered temporary jobs on definitely less advantageous terms than is normal. New segments of the labor market then develop, or new activities appear which do not operate in accordance with normal rules.[9] How far these adaptations can go in reducing unemployment is debatable. But they are part of present economic reality and should, therefore, be seriously studied by economists.

Some Questions for Dynamic Analysis

The preceding survey of the three main sources of spontaneous evolution in an economy experiencing mass unemployment suggests which features should be incorporated in our ideas about medium- and long-term developments. To these ideas, to the models within which they can be formalized and tested, and to the theories that they support we must now turn our attention.

1. An opening comment has to be made. We are confronted with a phenomenon whose dynamic analysis is necessarily either quite partial or quite complex. Realizing this fact, and considering how imprecise is our econometric knowledge of very significant aspects of the phenomenon, we must be modest in the presentation of whatever

---

[9] This phenomenon has been well described taking the particular example of France by M. Piore, "Dualism in the labor market: a response to uncertainty and flux. The case of France," *Revue Economique* (January 1978). On the experience of the USA and other countries, see also S. Berger and M. Piore, *Dualism and Discontinuity in Industrial Societies* (Cambridge: Cambridge University Press, 1980).

we think we have understood. The mathematical analysis of economic growth under instantaneous and permanent market clearing, with perfect competition and self-fulfilling expectations provides a useful, although somewhat remote, point of comparison. It has been worked out only recently and the results that have been proved, for instance with respect to stability, are not clearcut; an econometric analysis would still be required in order to decide which of the many conceivable cases are the most relevant ones for us.

With respect to this point of comparison we have to introduce disequilibria, imperfections in competition and realistic patterns for expectations. We have to represent the sluggishness in price changes, in labor and capital mobility, as well as in other adjustments of production, consumption, investment and anticipation. We must leave room for exogenous shocks concerning the economic and political environment, or even simply "animal spirits." The prospect of having to master these many aspects, and eventually all at the same time, is overwhelming.

I believe that the difficulty of the challenge is well realized within our profession. But since economists are human beings they sometimes adopt attitudes that permit them to avoid the challenge. Among those attitudes the least objectionable is to give up and remain silent. Indeed, some of my colleagues consider that as economists we understand the phenomenon of mass unemployment too poorly to say anything at all about it to our fellow citizens. Some even think that we cannot make any significant progress in our understanding of the phenomenon and so they work on other, academically more rewarding, subjects. A different attitude is to deny the phenomenon and to argue, for instance, that, since any mutually advantageous move has to be made in our society by those benefiting from it, malfunctionings cannot occur and involuntary unemployment, therefore, does not exist. Still another attitude is to become charlatans and to advertize a simple remedy, for instance a fixed monetary rule, a so-called "supply-side" medicine or a protectionist package, the media being, as always, ready to contribute to giving such remedies favorable publicity at least as long as they look new.

Avoiding these various attitudes, being committed to intensifying our research on what is an important social problem and to transmitting with the appropriate modesty the partial results that we may hope to obtain, we still have to adopt a research strategy. On the dynamic analysis of unemployment, my own strategy has been to undertake quite tentative explorations, for want of a better alternative. I have specified very simple dynamic models, which I believe illustrate the relevant features of the phenomenon. I have then looked at the economic evolution possible from these models, paying particular attention to certain scenarios which I thought typical of what is happening today. I am aware that this type of exploration leaves much in the dark. Whatever results are obtained can claim no generality, they should rather be taken as provisional hypotheses to be further tested. However, when they seem to describe presently observed facts, I am inclined to grant them a more general validity than the particular specification from which they were derived.

It is in this spirit that I shall now approach a few questions that are worth studying if we want to be better equipped for discussing medium- and long-term evolutions, in particular those that may be induced by macroeconomic policies.

2. How long will mass unemployment last? This basic question is often asked in Western Europe. A similar question was raised in the USA in the thirties, and may

still be raised here today. In trying to answer it, we may conveniently divide it into two subsidiary questions: (i) Would the spontaneous evolution of the economy restore full employment? (ii) Under which conditions will economic policies help?

The feeling of many economists is that mass unemployment can only be transitory and that spontaneous economic adaptations will get rid of it. Others are less optimistic. In order to sort out our ideas about this question, we must consider whether or not we can make a theoretical case for a stable stationary state with an excess supply of labor. The question was indeed already posed in this way during some of the initial discussions concerning the validity of Keynes' *General Theory*. For instance, when A.C. Pigou wanted to stress the role of his famous wealth effect, he wrote an article entitled "The classical stationary state,"[10] arguing that excess supply could not be permanent.

Those who hold that a stable stationary state of excess supply is conceivable also think that the degree of excess supply depends on some exogenous factors that are, of course, held constant for any particular stationary state, but could have taken different values. There is, then, a full range of conceivable stationary states with a varying degree of unemployment. An explicitly dynamic setting is, of course, required for any discussion about the existence of such a range of stable stationary states with permanent excess supply. It is, then, surprising to realize that the theoretical literature is very scarce, as soon as we require it to be explicit in its dynamic hypotheses and rigorous in its dynamic analysis. I do not remember any reference to publications made before the seventies.

---

[10] A.C. Pigou, "The classical stationary state," *Economic Journal* (December 1943).

At present, a number of exploratory theoretical models are available, and they provide us with as many experimental schemes for testing our ideas. In some respects these theoretical models can also be seen as exhibiting features to be found in current macroecononometric models. For both these reasons they may deserve wider consideration and discussion than has occurred so far.

The answers given to the possible existence of stable stationary states of excess supply are of course sensitive to the specification that is chosen for the analysis, and more particularly to what is assumed about changes of the general levels of prices and wages. We may distinguish three classes of models in this respect.

In the first, the price system is taken to be completely rigid, at least for the characteristics playing a role in the formalization.[11] It is then typically found that other dynamic adjustments, such as those resulting from capital accumulation, are consistent with the existence of stable stationary states with permanent excess supply.

The second group of models assumes some downward flexibility of prices in cases of excess supply. More precisely, it assumes that the rate of change of the price level is an increasing function of the excess demand for goods. This implies that, in the case of Keynesian unemployment, price deflation tends to increase real wealth

---

[11] As an example of a model belonging to this class, see V. Böhm, "Disequilibrium dynamics in a simple macroeconomic model," *Journal of Economic Theory* (April 1978). Also relevant are two now classical articles: A.S. Blinder and R.M. Solow, "Does fiscal policy matter?" *Journal of Public Economics* (November 1973) and J. Tobin and W. Buiter, "Long-run effects of fiscal and monetary policy on aggregate demand," in J.L. Stein (ed.), *Monetarism* (Amsterdam: North-Holland, 1976). I may, finally, mention the model used in E. Malinvaud, "Wages and unemployment," *Economic Journal* (March 1982).

and, therefore, to stimulate demand. But this effect does not necessarily rule out the possibility of permanent unemployment. Indeed, a limit regime is often found in which the price level decreases at a constant rate, but real wealth remains constant because of the dissaving implied by a low level of activity. Real magnitudes then define a stable stationary state with excess supply.[12]

This second group of models, not to speak of the first, neglects the critique raised by M. Friedman against the simple expression of the Phillips curve.[13] It pays no attention to the revision of expectations that might follow from a sustained price movement. In other words, it assumes that, at any time, the rate of price deflation depends only on the size of excess supply and not on the past evolution of the price level. This is tantamount to taking price makers as holding the same expectations concerning each other's behavior, no matter what the past evolution of prices and wages has been. It is, then, rather unrealistic.

The third category of dynamic models includes those in which price changes are assumed to depend not only on excess demand but also on expected price changes, the rate of which may be taken to be directly related to the past rate of price increases. I know of only one publication in

---

[12] These models typically neglect the short-term depressing effect of price deflation coming from financial difficulties experienced by debtors. Needless to say, this depressing effect may actually play a very important role. Reference may be made to S. Honkapohja, "On the dynamics of disequilibria in a macro model with flexible prices and wages," in M. Aoki and A. Mazzolo (eds), *New Trends in Dynamic System Theory and Economics* (New York: Academic Press, 1979). See also E. Malinvaud, *Profitability and Unemployment* (Cambridge: Cambridge University Press, 1980), chapter 3.

[13] See, for instance, M. Friedman, "The role of monetary policy," *American Economic Review* (March 1968).

which such a dynamic model has been used for studying the question that I raised here. It is James Tobin's article, entitled "Keynesian models of recession and depression."[14] With the particular specification used in that article,[15] we find two situations: (a) if the expected rate of price changes has a strong impact on aggregate demand (i.e. if "the speculative effect," inducing postponement of purchases when prices are expected to decrease, is strong) while the level of prices has a weak impact (the wealth effect being small), then depressions are cumulative, a situation which is worse than a tendency toward a Keynesian stationary regime; (b) in the opposite case, the economy converges to a limit in which the excess supply or demand will be just at the level for which it is neutral in its action on prices. This second situation corresponds to what Friedman called the "natural rate of unemployment" but was later and more appropriately called the NAIRU, the "non-accelerating inflation rate of unemployment."

The present state of the literature on this major issue of the stability of the Keynesian depression is, as I said, still unsatisfactory. But it does give us some insights. When attention is paid to situations of excess supply, all three categories of models are worth studying because wages and prices are definitely less flexible downward than upward, so that adaptations induced through changes of the price level and revisions of the expected rate of price change are both slow. These models bring to the fore various reasons

---

[14] J. Tobin, "Keynesian models of recession and depression," *American Economic Review* (May 1975).

[15] The specification chosen by J. Tobin for the adjustment process of prices and output (what he called the "Walras—Keynes—Phillips model") does not seem to me to be the most appropriate (see E. Malinvaud, *Théorie Macroéconomique* (Paris: Dunod, 1982), chapter 8, section 2.1). In any case discussion of alternative specifications would be useful, considering the relevance of the issue.

explaining why depressing effects may be at times not only strong but also lasting. Even if a tendency exists that will spontaneously lead the economy toward a well-defined limit which does not depend on initial conditions concerning, in particular, aggregate demand, this limit itself, and the speed at which it is reached, may vary from one country to another, or from one historical period to another. Indeed, they depend on the dynamics of price and wage revisions, for which institutions and socio-political national factors are relevant. Friedman ventured to estimate that in the USA the spontaneous tendency toward what he called "the natural rate of unemployment" would take "say, a couple of decades."[16] The speed might well be much slower in economies in which market forces are less effective than they are in the USA.

3. I shall be more brief in discussing a similar question about the second extreme form of mass unemployment: How lasting can classical unemployment be? The literature is very scanty and the answer seems at first to be quite obvious. Excess demand for goods and excess supply of labor should induce an increase of the price level and a decrease of real wage rates, which would restore business profitability and lead firms to expand their operations until they are constrained by either lack of demand or lack of labor.

On further reflection we may, however, wonder whether this dynamic process works to the full extent that such an outline suggests. Economic historians take it as fact that profitability has remained low during some long periods and high during other long periods. They also believe that high profitability sometimes characterizes a fast-growing economy, while low profitability is maintained in a neigh-

---

[16] *American Economic Review* (1968), p. 11.

bouring less-fortunate economy, the difference persisting, again, for decades.

In my view, it would be worth studying growth models that would accommodate various degrees of profitability. Discussing them should help us to understand some features of sustained unemployment in slowly growing economies, in which a lack of profitability prevents expansion of productive capacities. In particular, we might study whether and under which conditions an economy can be trapped in a "supply glut."

We must also realize that it is possible to build simple theoretical models exhibiting stable regimes of classical unemployment, as soon as we suppose enough price rigidity. Such a result may be found, for instance, under full rigidity of real wages, a situation that was approximated recently in several Western European countries, or again if nominal wages are assumed to be drifting upward at an exogenously given rate and if price increases are expectations-insensitive, i.e. are not accelerating in the case of a stationary positive excess demand for goods.[17] Of course, these theoretical models should not be taken as applying exactly, since their hypotheses concerning, for instance, wage formation are caricatures, but they do suggest that classical unemployment may last longer than a classical economic training might lead one to think. It seems to me that the same conclusion follows from mathematical simulations that have been worked out within models relying on more realistic hypotheses in which the values of the relevant coefficients were chosen so as to be in line with econometric evidence.[18]

---

[17] See Malinvaud, *Théorie macroéconomique*, chapter 7, section 4.10.

[18] See Malinvaud, *Profitability and Unemployment*; and M. Bruno and J. Sachs, "Input price shocks and the slowdown of economic growth: the case of UK manufacturing," *Review of Economic Studies* 49 (1982).

For a study of mass unemployment, the relevance of classical unemployment extends beyond the question of knowing for how long it would last if it occurred in a pure form. On the one hand, we must remember the diversity of sectoral situations and admit that, except under very extreme circumstances, some degree of classical unemployment will always be present. On the other hand, even forgetting about this diversity, we must be concerned by what will happen when a phase of classical unemployment comes to an end. It is unlikely that a perfectly balanced equilibrium will be reached; I have even argued that the likely outcome will be prolonged unemployment, of the Keynesian type.[19] If this is correct, any worsening of unemployment when it is of the classical kind will also worsen the situation that will subsequently be left.

This argument may in fact be made quite simple. A low profitability will induce a low investment in the building of new productive capacities and, perhaps also, a high rate of scrapping of existing capacities. The productive capacity of equipment will then decrease or at least increase too slowly in relation to the growth of the productive potential of the labor force. Full employment will then become impossible. If classical unemployment ends, then only Keynesian unemployment can follow. A rigorous formalization of the argument must, of course, prove the various steps that I have just sketched and this is not done without introducing restrictive hypotheses. I believe, however, that the point is valid.[20]

---

[19] See Malinvaud, *Profitability and Unemployment.*

[20] Focusing attention on medium-term evolutions, the argument associates classical unemployment with a low profitability. But it has been shown recently that at the beginning of a fast recovery firms may be unwilling to expand output at the speed of demand expansion, because of adjustment costs concerning quick changes of their modes of production and of their labor force. This means that

4. A third question to be explored with the help of simple dynamic theoretical models concerns the conditions under which a policy of wage restraint will contribute to reducing unemployment.

Those in favor of such a policy usually stress the positive impact that higher profits will have on investment, because they mean that firms will have larger financial resources and because they improve profitability prospects. In order to be complete this argument should, however, show how lower wages will lead to higher profits and how a larger investment will lead to more employment. Neither of these two implications is taken as self-evident by all economists. So we ought to precisely sort out our ideas about them.

The argument would be quite convincing if unemployment could be assumed to be purely classical: a lower real wage would then stimulate a higher output by firms facing an excess demand for their products, and so immediately create higher profits and higher employment. The subsequent building of new productive capacities would clearly be favorable as long as unemployment remained classical. The theoretical problem is, rather, to know whether a policy of wage restraint can also be beneficial even in some cases when unemployment is Keynesian. Those in support

---

unemployment becomes classical although profitability then is typically good except for adjustment costs. This unemployment may disappear at a further stage of expansion, thus leading to a situation of generalized excess demand. This is a different case from the one considered above. Whether or not Keynesian unemployment will reappear, the phenomenon may explain why some demand-stimulation policies were at times said to have been too strong, not because they led to overemployment but because they induced a temporary excess demand for goods that stimulated price inflation. On this alternative situation see P. Artus, G. Laroque and G. Michel, "Estimation of a quarterly macroeconomic model with quantity rationing," forthcoming in *Econometrica*.

of such a policy may cite the favorable effects on aggregate demand, on capital—labor substitution or on competitiveness. Each one of these is worthy of close scrutiny.

For a reduction of wages to have a direct positive impact on aggregate demand, a propensity to spend from profits more than from wages is required. It is usually considered, however, that the opposite applies; so I shall not devote any time to examining more fully this first kind of argument. I shall consider that people who argue for lower wages, because higher investment would then stimulate aggregate demand, simply overlook the stronger depressing effect on consumption. I am ready to examine empirical evidence which claims to show that, in some circumstances at least, the sensitivity of investment to profits is so high that the commonly held hypothesis should be reversed, but I have not yet seen any.

A lower relative cost of labor with respect to capital induces a firm to choose a less capital-intensive technique of production and, therefore, to have a larger labor demand for any given amount of the aggregate demand for their product. The impact of a reduction of wages on unemployment then depends on two opposing factors: a decrease of aggregate demand, but an increase of labor requirement per unit of output. Which factor dominates depends, in particular, on the degree of capital—labor substitutability. There is now good documentation on the theory according to which this substitutability is quite small in the short term, for work on given equipments, with a given organization of production, but quite significant in the long term, when equipments are built or replaced, and when methods of production are reorganized. We can then imagine that the responses of employment to lower wages will be negative in the short term but positive in the long term.

This is, indeed, the conclusion to be drawn from the

dynamic responses that have been studied within a simple model in which the technology has the putty-clay feature.[21] Within the range of values of the coefficients leading to a realistic specification, the short-term increase and long-term decrease of Keynesian unemployment seem to be well established.

Consideration of the competitiveness of an open economy subject to a foreign exchange constraint reinforces the case for a wage restraint and also leads us to distinguish between short- and long-term results. This has been shown by J. Drèze and F. Modigliani[22] who assumed that government demand management is bound by a constraint on the balance of foreign trade. When competitiveness is low and the balance of payments deficit cannot be increased, the government must stick to a depressing demand policy, even when idle productive capacities are available. If competitiveness improves, a less restrictive policy can be introduced. Output and employment then increase while the trade deficit remains within the admissible limit.

Trying to evaluate how a policy of wage restraint, supplemented by an aggregate demand regulation of the above type, could contribute to improving employment in Belgium, Drèze and Modigliani argued that the main impact of profitability on unemployment goes through the effect on productive capacities. Neglecting the substitutability of capital for labor, they found that, with the assumed economic policy, the elasticity of employment with respect to the real wage was equal to something like

---

[21] E. Malinvaud, "Wages and unemployment," *Economic Journal* (March 1982).

[22] J. Drèze and F. Modigliani, "The trade-off between real wages and employment in an open economy (Belgium)," *European Economic Review* (January 1981).

−0.2 for given productive capacities, but could be evaluated at roughly −2 when the induced increase of productive capacities was taken into account.

Surveying the theoretical dynamic analysis of unemployment we are, thus, led to consider questions that come close to the study of public policies, which are the subject of the third lecture.

3　Policies and Institutions

The ultimate aim of economics is to provide guidance for action. It should help when institutions are set up or revised so as to permit a smooth and satisfactory functioning of our society. It should help when broad policy lines are chosen to cover several years, or even decades. Finally, it should also help in the economic regulation that has to be permanently made so as to improve current economic evolution. We must, therefore, consider it natural that economists are called for advice or even that they give recommendations when they are not called to do so.

The behavior of the profession is, however, not satisfactory in this respect. Since economics has become a science that non-economists are not able to grasp and evaluate for themselves, we should expect that any advice or recommendation made by economists is based on firmly established knowledge. The results or modes of analysis that are being used should have been proved valid, which means that they should be supported by a broad consensus of the profession. Direct transmission to policy makers of theses or hypotheses should be withheld until these have been properly tested and, therefore, accepted by specialists.

I need not dwell on the fact that in practice things are often different. But I may be permitted to say that I have been somewhat distressed by what I perceive to be the message sent during the last decade by American academia to policy makers throughout the world, not so much because the recommendations were at variance with those I would have given myself, but because I knew they were coming from a minority that was too easily given a leading voice in American universities. In any case, I shall plead for much more care and modesty when economists speak about policy matters.

This being my position, you understand that I approach the subject of this last lecture with great diffidence. Faced with the major social problem that mass unemployment has now become, I have not *the* solution, but rather some ideas as to how unemployment ought to be contained. Moreover, I recognize that some of these ideas are not widely held. They are, therefore, proposed to my economist colleagues for discussion. I do not present them as complete, still less as a program for public action.

Only a few of my ideas are direct consequences of the theoretical development surveyed in the second lecture. All of them, of course, fit with the general vision of mass unemployment being a disequilibrium. But I want, in this lecture, to present the full range of what I think I have learned from my experience with French and European economic policies. Thus, I do not feel I should be constrained by the limits that the discussion of a well-organized theory would otherwise impose.

Hoping that after these warnings I shall not be misunderstood, I shall proceed to the subject and make frequent references to the situation I know best, namely that of France and of Western Europe more generally. I shall first comment on the nature of the unemployment problem that challenges our society at this historical time. I shall then deal successively with short-term economic policies as they were viewed in the sixties, with actions intended to curb the evolution of relative prices, incomes and costs and, finally, with rules and decisions motivated by the prospect of a lasting phase of mass unemployment.

A section will be devoted to the relationship between unemployment and the choice of the economic system. The lecture will then end with a brief examination of the question, why past policies have not been more efficient in preventing us from reaching the present high levels of unemployment.

The Challenge

"There is too much unemployment now." This statement meets with almost universal consensus, both in Western Europe where during the last decade the trend in ever higher unemployment has been very strong and in the USA, where business fluctuations seem to bring the unemployment rate to ever higher peaks. Work is necessary for self-fulfillment. For a proportion of those who suffer from it, the lack of work also means poverty. By its concentration amongst young people and minority groups, unemployment also creates a new cause of social division and often acute conflict within our cities.

But we must be lucid and realize that we had little chance of achieving a better employment situation without cost, or of significantly improving employment prospects now without sacrifice. The statement, "There is too much unemployment," means that we feel that the cost should have been borne and that we are now ready to accept some sacrifice. There is necessarily a trade-off between employment and other objectives. Opinions vary about the best choice to make when considering this trade-off, but I cannot help feeling that a large majority of people would have given priority to employment if they had been given the option of so doing.

Even granting the great uncertainties in the present understanding of economic phenomena, many people believe that something could have been successfully done and that today it is again possible to take actions that will almost certainly be beneficial. As for myself, I have been observing rather closely for many years both the economic situation and the decision-making process in my country. I share the above view and consider it as a failure that economists have proved unable to convey to our fellow citizens a clear and convincing message of what ought to have been done. This belief is based on three convictions: that the rise of unemployment could have been foreseen; that some possibilities existed for coping better with it; and that the costs were worth bearing.

1. Before going any further we must, however, recognize the great lacunae in our knowledge of what unemployment really imposes on those who experience it and on communities in which it is serious. If policy makers are to be confronted with an objective and accurate evaluation of the real trade-off between employment and other objectives, we must know more about this.

It is known that, at any one time, those who are unemployed are a very mixed group and that the experience of unemployment will mean quite different things to different people. Some will find a job quickly, even in a few cases a better job than the one they were previously holding; others will quickly leave the labor force; but others still will remain unemployed for a long time. Some unemployed people live in households where one or more of their family members is gainfully employed, but others are not in this situation. A close look at the life-cycles of individuals or households would then certainly reveal a great diversity with respect to the impact that unemployment had on them. But it is also known that the risk of unemployment is quite unevenly distributed among the various social groups and that people who have once been unemployed are particularly at risk of becoming so again.

These considerations make it difficult to establish any statistical picture. The pictures now available have, moreover, a limited relevance because they typically concern rather short life-spans.[1] Ehrenberg and Smith comment, in particular, on the difficulties of evaluating the handicap in their adult life suffered by people who were unemployed when young.[2]

There is more documentation on the problem of knowing the income loss resulting from unemployment. A recent OECD survey shows that, for a good proportion of workers, the loss of a job means, for a time, only a limited loss of income.[3] The situation varies a great deal between countries. An aggregate indicator has been defined as the ratio between the average unemployment compensation received by unemployed persons and the average wage of a manual worker. Values of the order of 0.5 have been found for such countries as Canada, France and West Germany, while 0.2 appears to roughly hold for the UK and 0.15 for Italy and the USA. These differences are caused by different conditions of eligibility for unemployment compensation, by a different ratio between the replacement income and the previously earned income, and by a different period of time during which replacement income is granted.

One general characteristic of the compensation system is that it does not cover, or only poorly covers, people who have been unemployed for rather a long time (such as more than a year) or who are unemployed again after

---

[1] An exceptionally long life-span is covered for instance by the USA National Longitudinal Survey, which was used to examine the concentration of unemployment on men aged 49 to 59 during the four years 1965–8. See Clark and Summers, *Brookings Papers on Economic Activity* (1979).

[2] Ehrenberg and Smith, chapter 15.

[3] OECD, "The present unemployment problem" (1983).

working in an occasional job for a short period (this situation is more frequent in the USA than in Europe). Unfortunately, these cases are usually amongst the poorest social groups, so that the poverty cost of unemployment may still be high nowadays, notwithstanding the great changes that have occurred in this respect since the period between the two world wars.

Other dimensions of the cost of unemployment are more difficult to grasp. Discouraged workers who drop out of the labor force, although, under normal conditions, they would work on the labor market, suffer a loss of welfare, the evaluation of which is not easy. Psychological and physical disturbances suffered by some of those who cannot find a job when finishing school or who remain unemployed for a long time are also not precisely known. Some of the social costs resulting from involuntary idleness in urban communities are manifest, but again a general picture has not yet been established.

On the other side of the balance sheet, namely on measuring the reduction of unemployment that can be obtained from policies, the situation is, of course, still worse. Precise measurement would presuppose an accurate knowledge of the whole functioning of our economic systems. What we can reasonably infer from our limited knowledge is, however, not negligible, as this lecture aims to show.

2. The main cause of the present unemployment problem is, of course, the slowdown of economic growth, which is a world-wide phenomenon and a long-term one. After a long period of exceptionally fast growth,[4] the world economy

---

[4] See, in particular, M. Abramovitz, "Rapid growth potential and its realisation: the experience of capitalist economies in the postwar period," in E. Malinvaud (ed.), *Economic Growth and Resources: The Major Issues* (London: Macmillan, 1979).

has had to adapt itself to less buoyant activity. This was bound to create labor surpluses in some industries and some regions. The difficulties were magnified since they occurred precisely at the time when the increase of the labor force accelerated because of demographic factors, resulting mainly from the postwar baby boom, and because of the increasing participation of women. But the transition from the phase of exceptionally fast economic growth to a new historical phase was mismanaged. The world economy entered a period of disturbance and, given this fact in particular, the responses of national economic policies were inappropriate to cope with the predictable unemployment problem.

This is not the place for a serious analysis of the reasons why so many of us believe that the world could have experienced a somewhat less disturbed transition. Nor is it the place for a serious examination of what ought to be done now so as to contain the international disorder. On the other hand, this international background is such a major determinant of present mass unemployment that it cannot be ignored in this lecture. I shall, therefore, make a brief comment on it.

For twenty years, in the fifties and sixties, the international economy provided decision makers with a vast, expanding, and apparently secure, market which operated under rather strict but known rules. Many countries at times experienced more or less sustained balance of payments or other difficulties, but the corrective policies used did not adversely affect the generally favorable economic climate. Around 1970 tensions appeared, which progressively disrupted the prevailing economic order and introduced major sources of uncertainty. The reactions to these new conditions were varied.

To begin with, a number of firms accepted losses which they believed to be temporary and they did not reorient their activity. A number of countries attempted to sustain their domestic output by expansionary fiscal policies, accepting large deficits in public budgets. Floating exchange rates, together with the financial permissiveness resulting from petrodollars and the international monetary supply, supported ambitious programs in Eastern Europe and the developing countries, which often led to huge balance-of-payments deficits. But this could not last. In the late seventies or early eighties, most private and public decision makers realized that the most sensible option for them was to adopt a cautious attitude and to take increased safety measures so as to be able to face possible disturbances. Depressing factors then became dominant in the world economy.

We must, of course, not underestimate the overwhelming difficulties that would have confronted and still do confront any attempt to master the transition from one phase of international economic development to another. Tensions had to occur in order to reveal that the end of the exceptional growth was approaching. We should not expect that our countries could have found a smooth path to slower growth. Large variations of the price of oil, volatility of exchange rates, and excessive indebtedness probably had to occur. Moreover, it was to be expected that some political leaders from both industrial countries and the Third World would try to take advantage of any available international forum, thus making concerted action still more difficult than it has always been.

It seems, however, clear in retrospect that it would have been possible at least to do a little better than was actually done (or, for that matter, also to do still worse). Variations of the price of oil could have been better handled, inflations and exchange rate volatility could have been somewhat weaker, financial relations could have been a little less disturbed.

The first condition for an improved management of the transition at the world level is the recognition of the problem and the will to do something about it. More and more economists and politicians have come to recognize the problem and propose steps to curb it. But others, particularly in the USA, claimed for too long that the problem was negligible and the market economy, if left alone, could resolve it in the best possible way. Although there is, of course, no simple solution, the advanced countries ought to rediscover the Bretton Woods spirit and the will to set up better international institutional arrangements than the one prevailing today. This being said, I shall from now on limit my attention to national policies and begin with the consideration of macroeconomic policies as they have been conceived and discussed during the past twenty-five years.

Demand Management and Short-term Actions

1. If the objective of economic policies had remained only improvement of the situation in the short term, then we should still be recommending essentially what was taught in the sixties about economic stabilization, i.e. counter-cyclical demand management. For short-term results, this approach appears to me to be validated by the outcome of theoretical reflection, econometric research and experience with economic policies.

Demand expansion engineered by budgetary or monetary policies always stimulates output for more than a year. There is usually some crowding out and the multiplier is smaller than simple models would predict, but this fact was already well recognized in the sixties. The behavior and anticipations of economic agents are never such as to lead them to quickly restrict their demands by the amount of what directly results from the initial stimulation. Indeed, the many macroeconometric models that now exist throughout the world agree on the direction of this short-term effect and even on the approximate magnitude of the corresponding multiplier. They differ substantially in their description of some behavior and of some adjustment processes, for instance of investment behavior and nominal wage formation, but these differences really matter only for effects appearing after two years or so.

Similarly, theoretical reflection has drawn attention to a number of hypotheses that were implicit in the teaching of the sixties and that might be restrictive: the existence of some profitable spare capacity, sluggishness in the revision of anticipations and so on. But careful examination of each of these hypotheses shows them to be admissible in the short term.

While it has significance for a number of issues, the literature of the new macroeconomic theory, with its outrageously simplified models and hypotheses, must not be taken at face value. This should be quite obvious to anyone who carefully compares these models and hypotheses with the large body of evidence contained in the well-documented macroeconomic data which now cover at least thirty years for a large number of countries.

This does not mean, of course, that demand management was always sensibly arranged, even from a limited short-term point of view. In some cases, stimulation or restriction came at the wrong time. In other cases, the increase of autonomous demand was too sharp. But such mistakes have nothing to do with the understanding of economic phenomena unless one adheres to a theory of capricious government that cannot be relied upon for any-thing.

At this stage we must conclude that it is, indeed, often possible to do something about unemployment in the short term by demand stimulation. But what can be done in this way is not very interesting if it cannot be repeated over a long period, or worse still, if it has perverse medium-term effects. Gaining a few decimal points on the un-employment rate of the following year cannot be the dominant and final objective of a policy intended to solve the unemployment problem.

2. It thus appears today that critics of Keynesian policies, Milton Friedman in particular, were right in stressing the need for a study of the longer term effects. For instance, if the favorable impact of a demand stimulation on employ-ment is only temporary and turns, after two years or so, purely into an acceleration of inflation, the situation may in the end be worse than it would otherwise have been.

Economic policies might, then, be evaluated within a broader context as parts of government *strategies* for regulating the economy. A strategy is defined with respect to the continuous observation of some variables that cannot be fully controlled; it tells how the government must react to this observation. More precisely, it gives a rule for the values that the policy instruments must take as a function of the values taken by observed variables. If monetary and fiscal instruments of the traditional type are used alone, a strategy of aggregate demand management is then defined. A research program might aim at finding out whether a strategy of this type exists that would stabilize the economy, which means that it would suf-ficiently reduce the size of business fluctuations for un-employment to remain at tolerable levels at all times.

While such a research program is of course valuable, the prospects of it providing the appropriate response to our present difficulties are bleak, for two reasons. First, with respect to solving the unemployment problem, it is no longer considered sufficient to dampen business fluctuations of rather short duration, corresponding to cycles of three to ten years. Second, our representations of the economic system are too imperfect to provide us with a reliable evaluation of definitive alternative strategies.

Reducing the size of business fluctuations would, undoubtedly, contribute to curbing unemployment, because it would reduce uncertainties about future economic evolution and thus make required profit margins smaller, which would at least lower the classical component of unemployment. This is precisely the reason why Europeans request the emergence of an international monetary system that would help to stabilize exchange rates. But dampening business fluctuations is no longer viewed as sufficient. On this issue views may be different in the USA from those in Western Europe. Present American unemployment may still be considered by many economists to result only from the fact that the US economy is just recovering from a business cycle trough. Beyond short-term fluctuations which are, of course, also present there, the rise of European unemployment is considered to be a long-term phenomenon. But the difference should not be overstressed: even in the USA a trend toward higher unemployment seems to exist and to exceed what could be attributed to an increase of frictional unemployment.

Against this background, the relevant picture of the working of the economic system is no longer that of a stable process, which is certainly subject to random shocks but which would otherwise spontaneously and rather quickly tend to full employment. The objectives of stabilization policies can no longer be viewed as being only to minimize the short-term negative employment effects of these shocks and to simply accelerate the spontaneous tendency to a return toward full employment. Other types of representation of the economic system are required, which allow for the possibility of lasting underemployment.

On the other hand, the study of government strategies is much more demanding with respect to the knowledge of economic phenomena than was the study of an isolated corrective policy. It is so demanding that economists may doubt whether we are today able to reach any firm and objective conclusion. Indeed, the alternative demand management strategies proposed and promoted by some critics of Keynesian policies have not been proved to be preferable and have not even been subject to rigorous scrutiny within models that could claim to provide an accurate representation of economic phenomena. Whereas the critics sometimes pointed to quite real difficulties, the counterproposals were never very well substantiated.

We should not fool ourselves. Some very good questions have been raised, such as how expectations are formed, how they affect behavior and therefore interact with other more commonly explored variables, how behavior changes after a change in government strategy, or under which conditions fixed rules for economic policy may be better than discretionary rules of a particular type. But the answers to these questions are not yet known. The discussions so far have been put within the framework of a few prototype models that cannot claim to provide even a first approximation to reality.[5] The present research on stabilization strategies should, therefore, be considered as the beginning of a long investigation that will still have to go through many stages before it can reach seriously founded conclusions to be used by policy makers.

Nor can we confidently rely on simulations made with the help of macroeconometric models or of fitted multi-

---

[5] This comment applies, in particular, to the small macroeconomic model consistently used in the rational expectation literature.

dimensional autoregressive representations that have recently been proposed as an alternative to econometric models. We know that different models have different dynamic properties and quite different long-term multipliers without any one of these models being recognized as more realistic than the others. Simulations of the same strategies on two models will, therefore, often lead to different conclusions. Autoregressive representations have not been experimented with enough for us to know well how they will contribute to our understanding of economic phenomena,[6] but I do not believe they will eventually be found to be superior to econometric models for the analysis of medium-term economic policies or for the study of the performances of alternative strategies.

3. Granted that we must look beyond short-term results and that our present knowledge is limited, how can we help in the choice of demand management policies with the purpose of curbing unemployment?

The main consideration to keep in mind is that demand expansion stimulates not only output but also balance of payments deficit and inflation. Whenever these secondary effects are significant, they will have to be corrected later on and it is unlikely that this will be done without damaging employment. Short-term economic policies must, then, be chosen with the concern for medium-term consequences and with the purpose of minimizing, over a number of years, the secondary effects that will have to be accepted when demand management is expansionary.

We know that these secondary effects will be all the more important in the following circumstances:

(a) when the capacity margin is smaller and more unevenly

---

[6] See C. Sims, "Macroeconomics and reality," *Econometrica* (January 1980).

distributed among firms, because bottlenecks will then play a larger role;

(b) when the increase in demand is more sudden, because the presence of short-term adjustment costs will then lead firms to increase prices and to accept the risk of losing market shares at the same time as they expand output and employment;

(c) when business finances are less healthy, because firms will then think first of restoring their profit margins before thinking of expanding.

Demand management will remain the main tool of short-term regulation. We now understand that it ought to avoid violent changes. The amount of expansion or contraction that it has to engineer must be evaluated in each particular case, due consideration being given not only to the current level of unemployment, but also to the stage reached by the inflationary process and to the specificities of its operation, as well as to the fundamental situation of business finance and profitability. When unemployment is massive, capacity margins limited, permanent acceleration of inflation almost institutionalized and profitability deeply deteriorated, short-term regulation and demand management face unsolvable dilemmas. More fundamental policy changes are required.

Actions on Prices, Incomes and Costs

Attention, then, naturally turns to the second type of policy considered by recent theoretical analysis, in particular by disequilibrium theory, namely direct action on the formation of costs and profit margins. This is all the more natural as the disequilibria associated with unemployment seem to exhibit, at least in Western Europe, new features which call for corrective intervention. Before discussing this diagnosis and various policy measures, we must realize the difficulties of an objective treatment of the issues involved. Let me first recall some basic issues.

1. As I have argued in the second lecture, we cannot expect the spontaneous evolution of prices to lead quickly to what would be required by full employment. Price disequilibria can be lasting, so they should concern policy makers who have some degree of freedom to act on them.

Any action should, of course, start from a diagnosis of what is wrong in the system of prices and remuneration rates that would otherwise tend to prevail in the medium term. In this respect two macroeconomic dimensions deserve particular attention. They concern the relative cost of labor with respect to capital and the profit rate earned on productive operations, relative to the real interest rate earned on loans. They are precisely the dimensions that matter for understanding investment behavior, for reasons given in the second lecture.

Deviations of the price system from what would be appropriate for medium-term growth originate from the complex process of macroeconomic dynamics, which involve behavioral reaction as well as historical experience and institutional characteristics. These deviations are, therefore, likely to change from one epoch to another, and from one country to another. Indeed, judging from the data presently available, it appears that international disparities concerning the macroeconomic characteristics of the system of relative prices are important, probably more so than international disparities in output growth rates.[7] Diagnosis of what ought to be corrected in these

---

[7] This conclusion may be drawn for instance from the data discussed by J. Sachs in "Real wages and unemployment in OECD countries," *Brookings Papers on Economic Activity* (no. 1, 1983).

prices and remuneration rates may, then, fundamentally vary from one country to another, and from one period to another. We must, moreover, admit that this diagnosis is bound to be difficult, because precise determination of what the appropriate price system is at each historical time would require more statistical and economic knowledge than is currently available. Let us briefly consider this difficulty.

The appropriate price system may be defined as the system that would induce an optimal economic growth which, starting from the actual initial situation, would optimally lead to a balanced growth with satisfactory utilization of human resources. We may imagine that determination of this price system proceeds by three successive steps.

First, we may try to determine a kind of neoclassical balanced growth benchmark. Considering future trends of population and "technical progress," and taking saving and labor supply behavior into account, we can determine a reference growth path and its dual price system in which the pure profit rate would be nil, the interest rate being equal to the marginal productivity of capital and the unit labor cost equal to the marginal productivity of labor. A study of this benchmark may be enlightening. For instance, if we admit that the trend of technical progress has slowed down in comparison with what it was in the sixties, this is a reason for both a lower rate of capital accumulation and a higher capital intensity and, hence, a lower equilibrium real rate of interest.

Second, we could introduce consideration of the uncertainties about business conditions. Since these conditions are not well known, and since they will undergo irregularities both at the micro and at the macro levels, the reference growth path cited above cannot be real. Some firms will have excess capacity, some workers will not find the jobs they expected, at times the whole economy will be depressed. A better approximation to reality would then be provided by a stochastic growth path in which uncertainties, irreversibilities and disequilibria would be given their proper role. At this stage some stationarity concerning the stochastic features would be assumed in order to make analysis manageable. Such a stochastic growth has not yet been precisely formalized, so far as I know. It is fairly clear, however, that its price system would deviate in one important respect from the one associated with the neoclassical reference path, namely it would permit a positive mean pure profit rate because of the prevalence of risk aversion. Heuristic reflection on such a growth model leads, moreover, to the conclusion that the pure profit rate associated with the typical mean path ought to increase between a specification corresponding to the situation of the sixties and another one corresponding to the situation of the eighties. Indeed, the degree of business uncertainty has definitely increased.

The third step would concern the study of how the economy should operate its transition from the current situation, and in particular from the current price system, to the typical stochastic path determined in the second step of the analysis. I have only vague ideas on how this last step should proceed and on what it might imply for the evolution of the price system. But, thinking that the goal of the exercise is to define corrective interventions intended to curb the current price system, I am ready to concentrate attention on a hypothetical transition strategy that would immediately enforce the price system determined in the second step, and be appropriate for conditions likely to hold in the future. It would then be assumed that quantities would progressively adapt to the shift of prices and remuneration rates and the particular disequilibria imposed by the transition would not be taken as a cause for concern. (Needless to say, I do not claim optimality of this strategy; I just mean that I am ready to accept it for the "thought-experiment" that would permit the determination of the discrepancies between the current and appropriate price systems.)

Clearly, a wealth of econometric knowledge would be required for a precise determination of appropriate prices and remuneration rates along the above lines. Many features concerning behavior, labor productive potential and technical progress would play a role in the computation of the future medium-term rate of growth. Technical substitutabilities would have to be precisely known for a correct evaluation of the appropriate real interest rate. Risk taking in business investment behavior would also have to be known for a good evaluation of the appropriate pure profit rate. I do not need to dwell on the fact that our present econometric knowledge leaves much to be desired when faced with such an agenda.

It is, perhaps, less obvious that problems also exist in deriving from observed prices and remuneration rates the indicators that ought to be compared with those that characterize the supposedly appropriate price system. Indeed, the appropriate price system would concern relative prices and be obtained from a model in which the interference of taxation rules would not be particularly stressed. We ought then to compute, from existing data, an image of the current price system that would permit direct comparison with this appropriate price system. More precisely, we ought to determine indicators of real labor unit cost, real capital unit cost and real profit rates which, in an economy without inflation and taxation, would have led firms to make decisions that would have roughly the same aggregate results as the ones observed in the existing economy.

Compared with the above methodology for a good

diagnosis on how the prevailing system of prices and remuneration rates ought to be corrected, current practice leaves much to be desired. Indeed, it focuses attention on comparisons between present and past values of indicators that are not necessarily the most relevant ones. For instance, it is often claimed that wage rates are now too high because the wage share of the national income is significantly higher than it was before 1974. The wage share may not, in fact, be a reliable indicator for such a diagnosis; moreover, it is hazardous to assume that the appropriate wage share now has the value observed before 1974. (Was this value appropriate at the time? Has the appropriate level remained constant since then?)

2. Notwithstanding these methodological problems, and for lack of a better alternative, I am going to rely here on the quite imperfect measures that are now available and proceed to a discussion of the diagnosis that can be made about the situation prevailing in various countries. I will address in turn three statements about present disequilibria:

(a) the rate of utilization of equipment appears to be fairly high when compared with the degree of utilization of human resources;

(b) the relative cost of labour with respect to capital is too high;

(c) the profit rates are too low.

If the first statement deserves examination here, it is because it gives support to the argument that present unemployment is not purely Keynesian and therefore calls for corrective intervention on prices. Considering each one of these statements, I shall first deal with the case of France, which I have studied more closely, and then turn to the case of other OECD countries.[8]

In France before 1974 the rate of capacity utilization in manufacturing moved roughly in accord with a measure of the degree of tension on the labor market (the ratio between the number of vacancies and the number of unemployed people). But since then the two statistics have departed. As a result, in 1979–80 the rate of capacity utilization (82 per cent), although somewhat lower than during the years 1969–72 (84 per cent), was higher than during the period 1965–8 (80 per cent) when the unemployment rate was so much lower.

It appears that, during the past ten years the growth of capacity just kept pace with the growth of output, but the latter had to be depressed by moderation of aggregate demand precisely because increased stimulus would have often hit capacity and overflowed to foreign producers, a situation which the balance of payments could not sustain. Hence, the argument that the growth of productive capacity was too slow holds true.

The same shift of the relationship between capacity utilization and unemployment appears in some other European countries, notably in the UK and West Germany. There is some indication of a similar phenomenon in the USA but it is definitely weaker there. Moreover, since the American balance of payments does not seem to have imposed any constraint on demand management policy, it does not seem so valid to talk of an insufficient building of productive capacity there.

Data on the relative costs of labor and capital have not

---

[8] I shall not repeat my main sources as I go along. For France it is "Analyse macroéconomique des déséquilibres: la France des vingt dernières années," in E. Malinvaud, *Essais*. For other countries it is OECD, "The present unemployment problem" (1983).

been widely discussed. The existing data are, however, well worth considering; they suggest the following picture. As long as labor was scarce, substitution of capital for labor in the production process appeared to be required. Given the increasing trend of wages and other labor costs, lowering the cost of capital helped both to shift in the right direction the relative cost of labor with respect to capital and to sustain the profit rate. But the same policy was followed later on in France for some time while there was an increasing labor surplus. Actually, the relative cost of labor with respect to capital had been growing at roughly 4.5 per cent per year from 1963 to 1971. It increased by more than 40 per cent from 1971 to 1975 and remained roughly at this high level up to 1979. We may take this fact as being partly responsible for the mismatch that may now be observed: labor saving has been pushed ahead to such an extent that a high degree of capacity utilization still implies a high unemployment rate. Since 1979 the relative cost of labor with respect to capital seems to have decreased somewhat, so that the distortion in the input requirements of newly built productive capacities may now be becoming less acute.

The data given by OECD for other countries are not as complete as those referred to above for France. They support, however, the same image of a fast increase of the relative labor cost until well into the seventies and of a decrease in recent years. It would, therefore, be interesting to look more precisely at these data and to study whether they explain the widespread occurrence in the seventies of a mismatch between input requirements and relative factor scarcities.

With regard to the second dimension of price disequilibria, namely the one directly concerning business profitability, it has often been said that the profit rate strongly deteriorated in the seventies. But this has also sometimes been disputed. We now have a number of estimates which, although imperfect in terms of the methodological discussion above, make the picture more precise.

In France the net profit rate of non-financial corporations, as usually defined in national accounting, oscillated slightly above 5 per cent from 1962 to 1973, declined and then rose again so that it was estimated at 2.5 per cent in 1979, and declined again so as to be close to zero in 1981 and 1982. But I should like to argue that this is not the most relevant measure to consider. What matters for stimulating investment in the building of new productive capacity is not the business profit rate as such, but the amount by which this rate exceeds the real interest rate. Moreover, the national accounting definition of profits should be corrected when inflation is significant. Whereas depreciation of physical assets is still correctly defined, depreciation of financial assets and liabilities is not. Indeed, the loss of purchasing power of outstanding debts is not taken into account. Since non-financial corporations are mainly debtors, they benefit from a capital gain that should be added to their profits, as usually defined.

When the correction for inflation is made on the French figures, the net profit rate appears to have been particularly high from 1968 to 1973 (above 7 per cent). During the last three of those years the real interest rate was quite moderate, so that the excess of the corrected net profit rate over the real interest rate amounted to roughly 5 per cent, a level that was achieved in 1962–6 but not since then. Evolution after the first oil shock implied an acceleration of inflation that increased the capital gains of indebted corporations and depressed the real interest rate. In 1979 the corrected net profit rate still exceeded the real interest rate by 4 per cent. The picture was completely changed after the second oil shock and the rise of interest rates: in 1981–2 the interest rate exceeded the profit rate by 2 per cent, a dramatic swing.

It thus appears that, in the French case, business profitability was not depressed in the early seventies, quite the contrary. It even stood up fairly well until 1979, although our measure may overestimate the significance of inflationary capital gains at that time. If it was expected that part of them was only a transitory windfall, future profitability may have been estimated at a somewhat lower level because of the prospect of receding inflation.

But the French case is a little special, as is shown by some OECD estimates concerning manufacturing industry. Of the six countries studied, only France and Canada did not experience a decrease of the gross profit rate between the late sixties and the early seventies. The decrease was quite significant in the other four countries, namely the USA, the UK, West Germany and Japan. On the other hand, in the USA and Canada, the recovery after the first oil shock restored profit rates to roughly the level that was achieved in the early seventies but this was not the case in the other countries.

The conclusion, then, is that national specificities may be quite significant when we consider the level and evolution of business profitability. If a central picture must, however, be drawn for the Western world, I might tentatively propose the following one. A first moderate decline of profit rates, as usually defined, occurred in the early seventies and a second moderate decline took place between those years and the recovery of 1978–9. Acceleration of inflation, however, where it took place, helped to maintain business profitability. It is only in the early eighties, with the new depression, the rise in interest rates and the decrease of inflation rates, that business profitability dramatically declined.

To sum up this discussion concerning a diagnosis of

disequilibria during the seventies and eighties, we may say that there are, indeed, some indications of the truth of two propositions:

(a) stimulated by a too-high relative cost of labor with respect to capital, substitution of capital for labor progressed at a more than optimal speed;
(b) depressed by a too-low pure profit rate, the building of new productive capacities was slowed down too much.

Some distinction must, however, be made. Whereas the first proposition was probably true during most of the seventies, we may doubt whether it still holds in the eighties. The second proposition seems to have more force for the first few years of the eighties than it had before. On the other hand, both propositions seem to apply better to Western Europe than to the USA.[9]

3. Policies may be intended to make the system of prices and remuneration rates more appropriate to the actual needs of economic growth than it would otherwise be. They may then use instruments that belong to two broad categories: manipulation of tax rules and rates, and prices and incomes policies.

Fiscal instruments have, indeed, often been used with the direct purpose of stimulating either investment or employment. Changes of amortization rules and subsidies to investments have played an important role in lowering the cost of productive capital and sustaining the profit rate

---

[9] Several research workers have indeed stressed that different diagnoses should be given for Europe and the USA. See, in particular, Sachs, *Brookings Papers on Economic Activity* (1983); M. Wegner, "The employment miracle in the United States and stagnating employment in the European Community: a tentative explanation," Commission of the European Communities, *Economic Papers* 17 (July 1983).

during the sixties and seventies. Similarly, subsidies to employment-creation schemes were often advocated and introduced in the seventies. Actually, in some countries the taxation system has been made so complex by such intervention that it is difficult to know now what the net impact of all the measures has been.

I do not want to make here any precise proposals for a taxation system that I would recommend as contributing to solving the problem of unemployment.[10] Clearly, if in a particular country the prospect is that the relative cost of labor with respect to capital will remain too high for many years, a shift of taxes from labor to capital would be advisable. But I should like to make three general points.

First, theoretical discussions about tax reform should not nowadays be limited to the examination of models in which market clearing is assumed permanently to hold. In particular, lasting mass unemployment is such an important feature of economic reality in some countries that it must be explicitly introduced both in the specification of the model describing the economic system and in the objective function.

Second, we should be clear just what can be achieved by taxation policy. It may be used as part of demand management in order to regulate the timing of some expenditure. What concerns us here is, however, different, namely whether taxation rates and rules should be used in order to change for a period of some time the relative factor costs or business profitability, so as to induce better medium-term decisions by firms. Such changes cannot be made

---

[10] I may, however, draw attention to a particular macroeconomic exercise concerning the French economy and reaching the conclusion that an increase in the taxation of energy would much contribute to containing French unemployment. See E. Raoul et al., "Les voies étroites d'une stratégie pour l'emploi," *Economie et Statistique* (June 1983).

often, and require some time for their implementation. Moreover they cannot go too far, since too strong an interference in primary income distribution would introduce unwanted distortions at the micro level.

Third, after many years during which measures were introduced piecemeal one after the other, a complete re-examination of what the taxation system does would be advisable in many countries.[11] Even though many of these measures were actually motivated by the concern about some aspect of the unemployment problem, it is not obvious to me that the end result is today favorable to employment. In particular, we cannot analyze the impact of subsidies without taking into account the compensating taxes financing them.

We might argue that, in Western Europe, the system of taxes and of social security contributions was set up after the war when a shortage of labor prevailed and was then adapted to this disequilibrium. During the last two decades, as the situation progressively shifted to one of labor surplus, some corrections were made in fiscal rules. But, as a result, the system lost its inner logic and needs to be put straight again on a new basis, better adapted to the situation of the eighties.

Income policies exist more or less permanently in most Western countries, since governments state objectives concerning the rate of inflation and some main indicators of income distribution, and since they use some of their power for direct interference within the process of prices and incomes formation, sometimes within "consensual tripartite negotiations," also called "social contracts."

---

[11] This sentence was written before I read M. King's progress report of the project launched by the National Bureau of Economic Research on the taxation of income from capital (see *NBER Reporter* (Cambridge), Fall 1983). I did not think I was so right.

Such policies are particularly relevant if actual prices and remuneration rates deviate from their appropriate values; it then makes sense for governments to aim at reducing the size of the deviation.

It makes all the more sense if one agrees with M. Bruno and J. Sachs when they argue that differences in historical and national experiences concerning these deviations are the result of structural and institutional differences affecting the dynamic process of prices and incomes formation.[12] The same macroeconomic shocks imply different reactions of the price system in different countries, depending on what are rules, customs and other factors affecting decisions on wages and prices, as well as the behavior of workers, business and government. The same anomalies of relative prices and remuneration rates persist for a greater or lesser length of time depending, for instance, on what kind of indexation prevails. It is quite understandable that public policies aim to improve the whole process.

But precisely because historical and national specificities matter and because the degree of freedom of a democratic government depends very much on circumstances, we cannot say in the abstract how incomes policies should operate, or even what they are able to achieve. It is up to the people in charge in a given country at a given time to decide what to do, once they have a reliable diagnosis of what is wrong.[13]

---

[12] See Sachs, *Brookings Papers on Economic Activity* (1983) and M. Bruno and J. Sachs, *Wages, Profit and Commodity Prices: Macroeconomics of Stagflation*, forthcoming. On a French contribution to the same view see R. Boyer, "Les salaires en longue période," *Economie et Statistique* (September 1978).

[13] This is the lesson to be learned from the very extensive survey of European experience, recently made by R.J. Flanagan, D.W. Soskice

How to Cope with a Lasting Disequilibrium

Realizing that mass unemployment is still likely to last for a number of years, we are led to wonder whether we cannot cope with it by actions other than those intended to reduce the size of disequilibria existing in the price system. Indeed, discussions in Western Europe, particularly in France, have also considered two types of institutional changes, concerning rules for public productive decisions and labor regulations. I will now examine them in turn, before wondering for how long we should plan to have to live with the same major disequilibrium.

1. Decisions concerning public utilities, regulated industries and publicly owned firms can use criteria other than the ones supposed to rule private productive decisions. Maximizing the net discounted profit computed from the existing price system is not necessarily the best rule to follow, for a number of reasons that have been well identified under the general heading of "failures of the price system." It is well known that, in a mixed economy, public decisions may have to adopt "second best" rules. The definition of these rules must take into account not only how the private economy operates and what are the social objectives, but also what is the set of policy instruments available to the public sector.[14]

In France, where the public productive sector is important, the examination of criteria to use is an old

---

and L. Ulman, *Unionism, Economic Stabilization and Incomes Policies: European Experience* (Washington: Brookings Institution, 1983).

[14] For a general treatment of these issues see, for instance, K. Arrow and M. Kurz, *Public Investment, the Rate of Return and Optimal Fiscal Policy* (Baltimore: Johns Hopkins Press, 1970).

tradition among economists, planners and managers of public firms. In particular, the discount rate for public project evaluations has been centrally determined for the past twenty years. It is, then, quite natural that important discussions recently occurred on whether and how the existing criteria used by public firms could be revised, so as to better take into account the fact that the private economy is experiencing mass unemployment.

We should not be surprised to learn that the discussions were often heated. Indeed, the choice of appropriate second best rules requires agreement not only on the objectives to be achieved by economic policy but also on a model of the actual working of the economic system. In France, however, still more than elsewhere, opinions vary a great deal about how this system actually works. It is noteworthy that, notwithstanding this fundamental difficulty, a special committee, representative of a wide spectrum of opinion, was able to conclude a report on what rules ought now to be followed.[15]

This is not the place to describe in detail the recommendations of the committee nor the various analytical papers on which they were based. What was achieved was not very original. To get a flavor of it we just have to know that some macroeconomic simulations on major productive choices were recommended, together with the use of shadow prices on smaller public projects, these prices somewhat lowering the labor cost and raising the exchange rate with respect to what they actually are at present. (Needless to say, the application of such shadow prices is much less rough and blind than direct quantitative targets

---

[15] "Calcul économique et résorption des déséquilibres" (Report of the Working Group on Economic Calculations, chaired by E. Malinvaud and R. Guesnerie) (Paris: Commissariat Général de Plan, November 1983).

concerning employment, exports or the use of inputs with large import content.) The main point is, rather, to stress the importance of the issue which is, of course, already well recognized by development economists.[16]

2. Labor regulations may take the disequilibrium of the labor market into account. They may even be directly motivated by the wish to reduce this disequilibrium. When mass unemployment occurs and is believed to be long-lasting, they may be intended to lower the labor supply. This is clearly so in a number of cases, particularly for the rules governing the immigration of foreign workers. I need not expand on this and discuss, for instance, how immigration was stimulated in the fifties and sixties, while it is now restricted. But two other types of direct controls are worthy of serious scrutiny: (i) regulations intended to induce groups of the population to take only a partial participation in the labor force; and (ii) regulations concerning the time at work.

Confronted with the challenging problem of unemployment, some people have suggested increased possibilities for the development of part-time jobs and for periods in active adult life devoted to education or leisure.[17] Prevailing labor regulations in some countries of Western Europe are, however, often considered to be unfavorable to such a limited participation in the labor force and it is actually less frequent in those countries than, for instance, in the

---

[16] The reader may find interest in studying the theoretical treatment of the problem in P. Picard, "Prix fictifs et déséquilibres en économie ouverte," *Cahiers du Séminaire d'Econométrie*, no. 25 (Paris: Centre National de la Recherche Scientifique, 1984).

[17] On arguments in favor of such schemes see L. Emmerij, "The social economy of today's employment problem in the industrialised countries," in Malinvaud and Fitoussi (eds), *Unemployment in Western Countries*.

USA. The motivations behind these proposals are often a bit obscure because the people suggesting them clearly think they would contribute to social progress quite independently of any effect on unemployment. Similarly, the lack of enthusiasm shown by trade unions leaders must be explained by the fear of losing some control of workers for whom work would no longer be the main concern.

The question raised for economists by such proposals is, however, to know whether, and by how much, they would lower unemployment. Making limited participation in the labor force more easy may not only reduce the supply of workers who were already economically active, but also induce some supply from those who were inactive. The net result might just as easily be an increase as a decrease in the aggregate supply of labor. Only econometrics can tell what it actually is. Unfortunately, I do not know of any attempt to evaluate the reaction of labor supply to changes in regulations concerning, for instance, part-time work.

Reduction in the time at work has for some time been a much more prominent issue in France and, more generally, in Western Europe. It should be enlightening to consider the conclusions that result from the various studies and discussions.

The labor supply of the economically active population that is employed full-time can be decreased if the age of retirement is lowered, if holidays are extended or if the working week is shortened. Changes in regulations concerning these three aspects have been discussed at length and some of them have been implemented. It is not suprising to find that serious examination by economists has confirmed the common sense point of view that such changes can contribute to the reduction of unemployment. But in order for them to do so to the largest possible extent, they should be chosen only after a full study of their consequences on the demand for labor. It is, indeed, conceivable that their negative impacts on this demand may compensate for the decrease of the labor supply.[18]

From this point of view, the main question is whether regulation changes increase production costs and by how much. If unemployment was purely Keynesian, this would not matter; attention would, rather, concentrate on any impact on aggregate demand for goods. But, in actual fact, unemployment is partly classical. An increase of production costs lowers the demand for labor, particularly in those firms whose profitability has already deteriorated, and there are many such firms in Western Europe now. On the other hand, aggregate demand is often constrained by balance of payments requirements. If reduction of unemployment is the only objective and if stimulation of the aggregate demand for goods has to be wiped out in some way, the extra cost due to regulation changes ought to be fully borne by the workers. For instance, if the working week is shortened, workers should not be fully compensated by an increase of the hourly wage rate. More precisely, their hourly wage rate ought to increase only to the extent that their hourly productivity increases. In practice, however, it is thought to be impossible to impose the full extra cost on the workers, at least not from the beginning, so that we must accept some negative impact on the demand for labor, unless business profitability is not a problem and there is some leeway for an expansion of the demand for goods.

It may be worth noting that precise examination of the problem has revealed a large variety of situations with

---

[18] See, in particular, G. Oudiz, E. Raoul and H. Sterdyniak, "Réduire la durée du travail, quelles conséquences?" *Economie et Statistique* (May 1979); Y. Barou and J. Rigaudiat, *Les 35 heures et l'emploi* (Paris: Documentation Française, 1983). See also the EEC report on this issue published in *European Economy* 5 (March 1980).

respect to the extra costs implied by regulatory changes. Some firms can change their modes of production with little extra cost; others cannot. If a reduction of the working week is imposed on those firms that cannot make the necessary accommodation they may have to bear a higher cost of capital per unit of output. They may even have to lower their output for lack of productive capacity. This leads me to recommend flexibility in preference to tight rules for the implementation of any change intended to lower the length of the working week.

3. A policy intended specifically to cope with lasting un-employment often raises suspicion from serious econo-mists. As far as I understand this reaction, it is one that fears that economic efficiency may be permanently damaged by remedies that are aimed at curing a temporary disease, namely mass unemployment. Economists fear that the use of shadow prices may be taken as an excuse by public managers for accepting losses and, therefore, being less scrupulous about expenditure. They also fear that an open policy of reduction of time at work might be inter-preted as an inducement to laziness and that a lowering of the retirement age might be irreversible when, in the twenty-first century, pension funds will experience a large permanent excess of payments over receipts unless the retirement age is raised.

Without going into any of these issues in detail, we must recognize the value of the general point. More precisely, most economists agree that, even though it will still last for some time, mass unemployment will also some day cease to be the general problem that it now is. No formal proof of this exists except the disputable ones that we briefly considered in the second lecture, but its intuitive validity is supported by reference to economic history, which shows that past periods of mass unemployment did end. When deciding about present economic policies, we should, then, not restrict attention to the present situation but also, sometimes, look beyond, especially when the measures contemplated have a structural character or concern long-range decisions. Nothing in our economic institutions is absolutely irreversible, but we know by experience that Keynes's famous sentence about the long run is dangerous when it leads to the neglect of everything except the proximate future.

Concern for what will happen after the present historical phase is important. In particular, if a shadow labor price is being used in public project evaluations, the limit up to which it is assumed to deviate from the actual price must be clearly set. Similarly, if fiscal rules are being changed in order to better adapt to a situation of excess labor supply, some attention should be paid to, and even probably some announcement made about, whether and how the rules ought to change again when the state of the labor market is more balanced.

My purpose here is only to raise the issue, which has scarcely been discussed and to which I have no definite answer. It should be more precisely looked into if the thrust of these lectures and of research along the same lines is to make any impact. When explicitly addressed, the question raises two reactions.

First, mass unemployment will last for some time. Indeed, taking the present difficulties of the world economy into account, Western European medium-term projections still show an increasing trend in unemployment for the next five years. If these projections are given credit, and frankly I do not see why they should not be, it is only during the nineties that we may expect Western European mass unemployment will recede.

Second, some people suggest that a kind of safety rule operates. Since measures intended to cope with mass un-

employment would by definition not be recommended if
the prospect was equilibrium growth, and since the limit
up to which the same kind of macroeconomic disequilibrium
might persist is uncertain, application of these measures
should be cautiously undertaken. If a kind of certainty-
equivalent limit is being used, after which equilibrium is
assumed, this limit should be somewhat sooner than the
mean expected duration of mass unemployment. I really
do not know whether this argument can be made rigorous
and convincing, but it seems to be worth considering.

The Economic System

Mass unemployment results from a malfunctioning of the
economy. When it is so long-lasting that it looks permanent,
the question naturally arises whether something fundamental in our economic system ought to be changed. Many
radical political attitudes have been motivated by this
question, even when what could come out of any contemplated revolution remains quite obscure. Devoting a
little attention to this general issue is not, therefore, out of
place, even if what I am going to say is not at all conclusive.

In fact it is surprising that there has been so little
scientific discussion of possible reforms to our economic
institutions that would reduce mass unemployment. Most
people probably intuitively believe that any change that
would bring positive results in this respect would also
imply other negative results which would make the final
outcome still worse. But when the stakes are important,
intuition ought to be checked, all the more so since it
might unexpectedly change.

It seems to me that three questions ought, in particular,
to be the object of serious scrutiny: Why is unemployment
low in Eastern Europe? How would the economic system

change in a country that would choose strong protectionism? Is unemployment in Western Europe partly due to an excessive rigidity of labour markets?

1. There are good reasons for the study of the situation in Eastern Europe. Indeed public opinion in some quarters, and a number of economists, believe that unemployment results from reliance on the profit motive, this being the prevailing criterion of economic decisions in our countries. It is then argued that public ownership of the means of production would result in the emergence of other criteria better suited to the common good. Eastern Europe provides an appropriate reference for an examination of this argument, even if experience there may also result from a totalitarian political regime that does not necessarily follow from public ownership and control of the economy.

Speaking of unemployment in Eastern Europe is rather difficult because of the lack of data. The claim that unemployment does not exist there at all is, of course, not true: there are people looking for jobs in these countries as well as in the West. That there is low unemployment there seems, however, to be generally accepted.[19] It is natural to relate this observation to the general situation of shortage that prevails in Eastern Europe. In the same way as excess supply of labor in the West is connected with excess supply of goods, excess demand for goods in the East occurs with high levels of employment. The same reasons that explain shortages on the goods markets also explain the better employment situation. If some kind of Eastern European managerial behavior is advocated in

---

[19] There are unemployment figures for Yugoslavia and they are high but one could say that this country is close to being a market economy. Examination of it deserves more space than I can give to it in this lecture.

order to solve the unemployment problem in the West, then we ought to understand precisely how an economy subject to such behavior operates, so as to be able to weigh costs against benefits.

Particular interest should then be given to the research program of Jànos Kornai and some of his Hungarian colleagues, which has been underway for a number of years.[20] It concerns the consequences of substituting quantitative production objectives for the profit motive and tight budget constraints, the latter characterizing Western rules of management. Disequilibria of a different type from those prevailing in the West are shown to result. Shortages tend to become predominant in most markets, forcing buyers to engage in new search activities, to accumulate precautionary stocks, to substitute inadequate inputs for unavailable adequate ones, or to give up some of their planned operations. A stable situation can then be maintained with such a degree of shortage intensity that it can reproduce itself from one period to the next one.

It is clear that this general framework alone does not answer all the questions that may be relevant. It has to be more fully formalized and studied. The final results of various managerial rules ought to be compared. The inefficiencies exhibited by the growth patterns obtained under such conditions ought to be appraised and, in particular, set against those observed in Western countries. But the framework is appropriate for putting into perspective the questions concerning the final normal impact of alternative management rules.

2. Faced with mass unemployment, and perceiving it as an

---

[20] See J. Kornai, *Economics of Shortage* (Amsterdam: North-Holland, 1980) and *Growth, Shortage and Efficiency* (Oxford: Basil Blackwell, 1982).

inescapable consequence of disorders in the world economy, some economists have argued in favor of a protectionist option that would insulate their countries.[21] Indeed, this option was very seriously considered, before being rejected, by the French socialist government. Any survey of economic policies intended to solve the unemployment problem must now consider this option. Clearly, it falls under the general heading of choices of economic system.

What is in question here must be differentiated from the limited protectionist measures that might sometimes be adopted in order to moderate strong and localized employment effects of aggressive foreign competition. Quite understandably, such measures have been adopted on certain occasions and no country can sincerely pretend to never use them. Indeed, even international trade agreements recognize that they are legitimate in some exceptional cases.

The option in question has a definite macroeconomic nature. Since a policy of aggregate demand expansion is barred by the balance of payments constraint, the proposition is to escape this constraint by restricting imports. In order to have a sufficient macroeconomic impact, restrictions must at least cover a substantial proportion of the

---

[21] It is not easy to find good references that would persuasively argue in favor of the pure form of this option. Those who are sometimes quoted as its supporters have often set important conditions for it to be successful, such as the requirement that protectionism be applied by the whole of Western Europe vis-à-vis the rest of the world or that some international understanding for the need of protectionist measures should exist. See in particular J.-M. Jeanneney, *Pour un nouveau protectionnisme* (Paris: Le Seuil, 1978); F. Cripps and W. Godley, "Control of imports as a means to full employment and the expansion of world trade," *Cambridge Journal of Economics* (September 1978).

import product mix. The common understanding of most of those advocating such a protectionist policy is that it would be applied by a particular country on its own. But the assumption of the passive response of other countries is not reasonable. Partners experiencing export losses as a consequence of the restrictions will retaliate in one way or another. The alternative to the present international economic system is, therefore, not one in which a single country protects iteself while freely exporting abroad, but either one in which most countries substantially restrict their imports if protectionist behavior is common, or one in which one country lives in isolation, restricting its imports but suffering counteracting restrictions on its exports. In the second case this would definitely mean a different economic system for the country involved.

It is, of course, difficult to evaluate the employment consequences of the isolationist option, because precise modelling would require some hypothesis on the extent of retaliation. (Who knows what it might be?) But my feeling is that, in order for the employment effect to be sizeable, the country would have to accept today a strong contraction of its foreign trade, and an important lowering of the volume of its consumption. I do not think this is what is wanted.[22] Nor can I imagine that people would prefer an economic system in which import restrictions were introduced spontaneously and independently by individual countries whenever they so desired. Clearly the initial disorder implied by such a system would greatly exceed the already substantial disorder that we now suffer with

---

[22] Reference to the German isolationist policy of the Nazi regime in the thirties might be worth discussing. In order to explain the size of the definitely favorable employment effect, we would undoubtedly have to examine also the impact of the aggressive German policy in Central Europe.

floating exchange rates, and employment would then react negatively. Eventually, international trade would have to strongly contract and the standard of living in the industrial world would go down substantially.

An alternative method of an internationally planned and orderly introduction of some import restrictions in selected countries that have a structural deficit in their foreign trade has been proposed.[23] It seems to me that a theoretical argument may be made for such an international policy if we accept the view that potential disequilibria in international trade (i.e. full employment disequilibria) can be lasting and that relative price rigidities exist that are not cured by devaluations. Such a view is indeed consistent with the one presented in these lectures. Proof of the theoretical validity of an international policy of the proposed type could be given along lines that would parallel those of an argument substantiating such domestic policies as restrictions to the inflow of foreign workers or reduction of the time at work.

---

[23] The proposition may be attributed to the "Cambridge Economic Policy Group" and was formalized by F. Cripps in "Causes of growth and recession in world trade," *Cambridge Economic Policy Review* (March 1978). A better reference may be the text and discussion of N. Kaldor, "The foundations of free trade theory and their implications for the current world recession," in Malinvaud and Fitoussi (eds), *Unemployment in Western Countries*.

Actually, the Cambridge group did not stress the need for international planning, as I do here. But careful reading of their writings and reflection on their propositions show that the intended results cannot be achieved without at least some international identification of which countries suffer a structural deficit, and some international understanding that these countries, but not others, are permitted to restrict their imports. I do not believe international agreements of this type can be reached without them being made quite explicit. To take just one example, does France suffer a structural deficit of its international trade?

But the problem is to know whether it is feasible to implement an international policy that would achieve the required economic adjustment. Considering the difficulties now faced by the monitoring of all international economic policies, even within the homogeneous group of countries constituting the European Economic Community, we must conclude that such a policy is still not feasible. It would require such a change in international relations that we cannot even entertain the hope of it becoming feasible in the near future.

3. The third question to be dealt with here concerning our economic system raises the issue of whether the rigidity of labor markets has not gone too far, at least in Western Europe.[24] This has, of course, been a consequence of clear social achievements, since it has followed from increased security given to the workers in their employment and real wage, and also from other types of labor protection. But considering the consequences, was too high a priority not given to these achievements?

Quite independently of any impact on aggregate employment, it can be argued that the need for labor input to adapt to changes of production was so neglected that the intended system proved to be untenable. In order to meet this need, new types of employment contracts were then developed, which gave very little security to the workers.[25] The dualism that resulted may appear socially unsatisfactory and unfair: the advantages and protection are granted to a majority of workers at the cost of quite unfavorable and insecure conditions for a minority. It seems impossible to make the system more equitable without

---

[24] The difference from the USA is worth stating again. See note 4 on page 46 and note 9 on p. 91.

[25] See, in particular, Piore, *Revue Economique* (1978).

reducing in some way the level of guarantee given to workers who are in the most secure positions.

Another way of stating this is by saying that present institutions imply a suboptimal distribution of jobs and earnings among workers. But it may also imply a suboptimal level of aggregate employment, for two reasons. First, the security granted to the worker often means a higher cost for the company. To the extent that unemployment is partly classical, this increased cost leads to a smaller demand for labor, unless compensation occurs, for instance by a lower wage rate. The argument outlined here may be made more precise and more specific for the various forms of worker protection that exist. Thus, the fact that in France and in the rest of Europe firms are constrained in their freedom to dismiss workers has recently been the object of a particular scrutiny. Broadly stated, the conclusion seems to be that such a scheme, of course, delays sudden decreases of employment but reduces the demand for labor by companies and is, therefore, unfavorable to employment in the medium- and long-term.[26]

Second, rigidity of the labor market increases the NAIRU, also called the "natural rate of unemployment," which is the rate at which the speed of inflation spontaneously tends to be constant. This is because rigidity reduces workers' mobility and, therefore, increases the duration of any mismatch between the supply of labor and the demand for labor. It is also because rigidity reduces the impact of market forces, so a higher level of unemployment is required to check the now-natural tendency of nominal wages to increase, and to do so at an accelerating rate when prices adjust accordingly.

---

[26] See, for instance, P. Krugman, "The real wage gap and employment," with discussion, *Annales de l'INSEE* (July–December 1982).

In order to maintain a constant rate of unemployment when the NAIRU increases, we should rely more on restrictive incomes policies. But in our economic system, incomes policies have only limited power; in order to have a good chance to succeed, they must be used with restraint by governments. Granted that rigid labor markets often have an oligopolistic structure that may help the implementation of incomes policies, we must, however, fear that this rigidity will finally force governments to stick to depressing demand management policies which are, of course, unfavorable to employment.

Why was Unemployment not Better Contained?

At the end of these lectures we may still look back and wonder why our economic policies failed to contain the rise of unemployment. To sort out our ideas on this question is important in more than one respect. It concerns, in particular, the crucial issue of knowing what role economists can play as policy advisers. Let us, then, examine in turn the possible validity of each one of the following four propositions:

(a) the coming increase of unemployment was under-estimated;
(b) the objective of reducing unemployment was not given top priority;
(c) there was not a sufficient consensus on a set of actions that would have been recognized as favorable to employment;
(d) favorable policy packages were ruled out as being un-implementable.

In Western Europe the increasing trend of unemployment could have been, and indeed, was, forecast.[27] It is, however, also true that most people underestimated the force of this trend. Macroeconomists who put forward disturbing figures for the unemployment rate, which subsequently turned out to be correct, were often treated as Cassandras. The common collective behavior was to reject disquieting forecasts, in the same way as forecasts of an approaching new war were often rejected in the late thirties in Europe.

But, whenever they recognized its existence, politicians claimed that the unemployment problem was their major concern. The relative merits of alternative government programs for reducing unemployment were often the key issues in political debates on the state of the economy. Actually, it could be said that up until recently the political class was more concerned by unemployment than was the general public. Opinion polls seemed to show that the issue was less important than expected. High unemployment

---

[27] Indeed, in France the rise of unemployment *was* foreseen and brought to public attention in the journal *Economie et Statistique* published by INSEE. Since this institute belongs to the Ministry of Economy, one understands that the forecast was stated with care, but it was widely and less carefully echoed by the media. In the issue of July–August 1975, it was evaluated that unemployment for 1980 could be contained at 700,000 if the average annual growth rate for the period 1973–80 could be raised to 5.1 per cent, an achievement that was already considered as incredible at the time, but unemployment would rise to one million if the growth rate was only 3.9 per cent. It turned out that the growth rate for this seven-year period was 2.7 per cent on average and unemployment in 1980 amounted to 1,450,000. In the issue of October 1979 the increase in unemployment was forecast to be 150,000 per annum during the period 1978–85, for an annual rate of growth of 2.7 per cent. Until 1983 the average increase was 180,000 per year notwithstanding some labor market policy measures such as those favoring early retirement which were not taken into account in the above forecast, but the average rate of growth was only 1.6 per cent.

rates are tolerated without the social unrest that was anticipated and policy proposals that are said to be favorable to employment are only popular if they imply no sacrifice, for instance in the purchasing power of employed people. We might, then, conclude that, notwithstanding political speeches, the unemployment problem was, in fact, not given very high priority because other concerns often dominated.

I tend, however, to give much more weight to the fact that politicians did not know what to do. There was no consensus among their advisers as to the results to be expected from various measures. I have, in particular, a vivid memory of my failure to obtain the support of some learned experts when I tried to explain that, under some conditions, favorable results would follow from a reduction of the working week or from a shift of relative factor costs that would make capital less cheap in comparison with labor. This may be partly due to the fact that in my country economic education is much less widespread than elsewhere; but it is also true to say that the degree of consensus amongst economists is too low for us to complain that decision makers are not following our advice.

The misgivings of policy makers are apparent as soon as we consider what they actually did. The labor market policies adopted in OECD countries since 1973 have been broadly characterized by a sequence of moves during six successive periods, one type of move dominating in each period:[28]

(a) to induce firms to retain employees whom they would have otherwise dismissed;
(b) to suppress such inducements;
(c) to subsidize job creation;

---

[28] OECD, "The present unemployment problem" (1983).

(d) to set up youth training programs;

(e) to reduce wages or wage rigidities;

(f) to lower labor supply, notably in organizing early retirements.

Misgivings are also apparent when we consider the macro-economic policies that have been successively followed.

Finally, issues of implementability certainly played a larger role than was explicitly stated. The risk of seeing a sensible policy package being distorted by the political process through which it had to pass was often felt to be great. For instance, proposed measures intended to lead to a reduction of the working week might, through this process, be supplemented by measures guaranteeing compensation for the loss of weekly pay, thus under-mining the efficacy of the proposal. Still more revealing are the misgivings over whether to reform the system of social security financing because, in this case, a fair degree of consensus existed among experts about the advisable direction of reform and many wondered whether the decisions finally taken would be completely different from the initial proposals. It was also feared that some of the contemplated changes would be taken to be permanent when they would only have a beneficial effect during a decade or so (the lowering of the retirement age is a case in point, particularly so with the peculiar age structure that two major wars have given to the French population).

The conclusion then is clear. Economics as a science has failed at this moment in history to convey to the general public a useful message on what ought to have been done in order to contain unemployment. Let us hope that in the future it will improve its ability to respond to some of the challenges posed by the evolution of our economies.

Index